A/78/17

General Assembly
Official Records
Seventy-eighth Session
Supplement No. 17

Report of the United Nations Commission on International Trade Law

Fifty-sixth session
(3–21 July 2023)

United Nations • New York, 2023

Note

Symbols of United Nations documents are composed of letters combined with figures. Mention of such a symbol indicates a reference to a United Nations document.

Print ISNB: 978-92-1-003419-7
eSBN: 978-92-1-107038-5

Contents

I. Introduction

1. The present report of the United Nations Commission on International Trade Law (UNCITRAL) covers the fifty-sixth session of the Commission, held in Vienna from 3 to 21 July 2023.

2. Pursuant to General Assembly resolution 2205 (XXI) of 17 December 1966, this report is submitted to the General Assembly and is also submitted for comments to the United Nations Conference on Trade and Development.

II. Organization of the session

A. Opening of the session

3. The fifty-sixth session of the Commission was opened by the Under-Secretary-General for Legal Affairs and Legal Counsel of the United Nations, Miguel de Serpa Soares, on 3 July 2023.

B. Membership and attendance

4. The General Assembly, in its resolution 2205 (XXI), established the Commission with a membership of 29 States, elected by the General Assembly. By its resolution 3108 (XXVIII) of 12 December 1973, the General Assembly increased the membership of the Commission from 29 to 36 States. By its resolution 57/20 of 19 November 2002, the General Assembly further increased the membership of the Commission from 36 States to 60 States. By its resolution 76/109 of 9 December 2021, the General Assembly increased again the membership of the Commission from 60 to 70 States. Five additional members were to be elected during the seventy-sixth session of the General Assembly, with the remaining five additional members to be elected during the seventy-ninth session of the General Assembly.

5. The current members of the Commission are the following States, whose term of office expires on the last day prior to the beginning of the annual session of the Commission in the year indicated:[1] Afghanistan (2028), Algeria (2025), Argentina (2028), Armenia (2028), Australia (2028), Austria (2028), Belarus (2028), Belgium (2025), Brazil (2028), Bulgaria (2028), Cameroon (2025), Canada (2025), Chile (2028), China (2025), Colombia (2028), Côte d'Ivoire (2025), Croatia (2025), Czechia (2028), Democratic Republic of the Congo (2028), Dominican Republic (2025), Ecuador (2025), Finland (2025), France (2025), Germany (2025), Ghana (2025), Greece (2028), Honduras (2025), Hungary (2025), India (2028), Indonesia (2025), Iran (Islamic Republic of) (2028), Iraq (2028), Israel (2028), Italy (2028), Japan (2025), Kenya (2028), Kuwait (2028), Malawi (2028), Malaysia (2025), Mali (2025), Mauritius (2028), Mexico (2025), Morocco (2028), Nigeria (2028), Panama (2028), Peru (2025), Poland (2028), Republic of Korea (2025), Russian Federation (2025), Saudi Arabia (2028), Singapore (2025), Somalia (2028), South Africa (2025), Spain (2028), Switzerland (2025), Thailand (2028), Türkiye (2028), Turkmenistan (2028), Uganda (2028), Ukraine (2025), United Kingdom of Great Britain and Northern Ireland (2025), United States of America (2028), Venezuela (Bolivarian Republic of) (2028), Viet Nam (2025) and Zimbabwe (2025).

[1] Pursuant to General Assembly resolution 2205 (XXI), the members of the Commission are elected for a term of six years. Of the current membership, 30 were elected by the Assembly on 17 December 2018, at its seventy-third session, 34 were elected by the Assembly on 15 March 2022, at its seventy-sixth session, and one was elected by the Assembly on 29 June 2022, at its seventy-sixth session. By its resolution 31/99, the Assembly altered the dates of commencement and termination of membership by deciding that members would take office at the beginning of the first day of the regular annual session of the Commission immediately following their election and that their terms of office would expire on the last day prior to the opening of the seventh regular annual session following their election.

6. With the exception of Bulgaria, Malawi, Mali, Mauritius, Nigeria and Somalia, all the members of the Commission were represented at the session.

7. The session was attended by observers from the following States: Angola, Bahrain, Bolivia (Plurinational State of), Bosnia and Herzegovina, Chad, Cyprus, Denmark, Egypt, El Salvador, Guatemala, Lebanon, Libya, Madagascar, Malta, Myanmar, Nepal, Netherlands (Kingdom of the), North Macedonia, Oman, Pakistan, Paraguay, Philippines, Portugal, Qatar, Romania, Slovakia, Sri Lanka, Sweden, Tajikistan, Togo, United Republic of Tanzania and Uruguay.

8. The session was also attended by observers from the European Union.

9. The session was also attended by observers from the following international organizations:

(a) *United Nations system*: World Bank Group;

(b) *Intergovernmental organizations*: Asian-African Legal Consultative Organization, Asian Development Bank, Eurasian Economic Commission, Hague Conference on Private International Law (HCCH), Inter-Parliamentary Assembly of Member Nations of the Commonwealth of Independent States, International Institute for the Unification of Private Law (UNIDROIT) and Permanent Court of Arbitration (PCA);

(c) *Invited non-governmental organizations*: Asia Pacific Centre for Arbitration and Mediation, Asian Academy of International Law, Asian International Arbitration Centre, Association for the Promotion of Arbitration in Africa, Beijing Arbitration Commission/Beijing International Arbitration Center, Cairo Regional Centre for International Commercial Arbitration, Center for International Investment and Commercial Arbitration, Centre for International Legal Studies, China Council for the Promotion of International Trade, China International Economic and Trade Arbitration Commission, European Law Institute, European Law Students' Association, Forum for International Conciliation and Arbitration, Georgian International Arbitration Centre, International and Comparative Law Research Center, International Association of Young Lawyers, International Bar Association, International Chamber of Commerce, International Commercial Arbitration Court at the Chamber of Commerce and Industry of Ukraine, International Federation of Freight Forwarders Associations, International Insolvency Institute, International Institute for Environment and Development, International Law Institute, International Rail Transport Committee, International Swaps and Derivatives Association, International Union of Notaries, International Women's Insolvency and Restructuring Confederation, Kozolchyk National Law Center, Latin American Group of Lawyers for International Trade Law, Law Association for Asia and the Pacific, Max Planck Institute for Comparative Public Law and International Law, Miami International Arbitration Society, Moot Alumni Association, Nigerian Institute of Chartered Arbitrators, PluriCourts, Russian Arbitration Association, Shanghai Arbitration Commission, Shenzhen Court of International Arbitration, Arbitration Institute of the Stockholm Chamber of Commerce, Tehran Chamber of Commerce, Industries, Mines and Agriculture, United States Council for International Business and Vienna International Arbitral Center.

10. The Commission welcomed the participation of international non-governmental organizations with expertise in the major items on the agenda. Their participation was crucial for the quality of texts formulated by the Commission, and the Commission requested the secretariat to continue to invite such organizations to its sessions.

C. Election of officers

11. The Commission elected the following officers:

Chair: Kathryn Sabo (Canada)

Vice-Chairs: Deborah Aba Aikins (Ghana)
Andrés Jana (Chile)
Siniša Petrović (Croatia)

Rapporteur: Mohammad Hossein Ghaniei (Islamic Republic of Iran)

D. Agenda

12. The agenda of the fifty-sixth session of the Commission as contained in the note by the Secretariat (A/CN.9/1121) was adopted by the Commission at its 1179th meeting, on 3 July 2023, as follows:

1. Opening of the session.
2. Election of officers.
3. Adoption of the agenda.
4. Consideration of texts prepared in the context of investor-State dispute settlement reform:
   (a) Consideration of draft codes of conduct for arbitrators and judges in international investment dispute resolution and respective commentary;
   (b) Consideration of draft provisions on mediation;
   (c) Consideration of draft guidelines on investment mediation.
5. Consideration of draft guide on access to credit for micro-, small and medium-sized enterprises.
6. UNCITRAL Colloquium on Climate Change and International Trade Law.
7. Consideration of the draft guidance text on early dismissal and preliminary determination for inclusion in the UNCITRAL Notes on Organizing Arbitral Proceedings.
8. Progress reports of working groups.
9. Coordination and cooperation.
10. Secretariat reports on non-legislative activities:
    (a) Technical assistance, cooperation and activities to support the use of UNCITRAL texts;
    (b) Status and promotion of UNCITRAL legal texts and the New York Convention;
    (c) Relevant General Assembly resolutions;
    (d) Current role of UNCITRAL in promoting the rule of law;
    (e) Bibliography of recent writings related to the work of UNCITRAL.
11. Work programme of the Commission.
12. Date and place of future meetings.
13. Other business.
14. Adoption of the report of the Commission.

E. Establishment of the Committee of the Whole

13. The Commission established a Committee of the Whole and referred to it for consideration agenda item 4 (Consideration of texts prepared in the context of investor-State dispute settlement reform). Considering the significant roles that the Chairperson and the Rapporteur have in the current project of Working Group III, the Commission elected Shane Spelliscy (Canada) and Natalie Yu-Lin Morris-Sharma (Singapore) as the Chairperson and the Rapporteur of the Committee of the Whole, respectively, in their personal capacity. The Committee of the Whole met from 3 to 7 July 2023 and held 9 meetings. At its 1188th meeting, on 7 July 2023, the Commission considered and adopted the report of the Committee of the Whole and agreed to include it in the present report. (The report of the Committee of the Whole is reproduced in paragraphs 25–34, 36–39 and 41–89 of the present report.)

F. Adoption of the report

14. The Commission adopted the present report by consensus at its 1188th meeting, on 7 July 2023, and at its 1204th and 1205th meetings, on 21 July 2023.

III. Summary of the work of the Commission at its fifty-sixth session

15. With respect to agenda item 4 (Consideration of texts prepared in the context of investor-State dispute settlement reform), the Commission finalized and adopted: (a) the UNCITRAL Model Provisions on Mediation for International Investment Disputes, which is reproduced in annex I to the present report; (b) the UNCITRAL Guidelines on Mediation for International Investment Disputes, which is reproduced in annex II to the present report; (c) the UNCITRAL Code of Conduct for Arbitrators in International Investment Dispute Resolution, which is reproduced in annex III to the present report; and (d) the UNCITRAL Code of Conduct for Judges in International Investment Dispute Resolution, which is reproduced in annex IV to the present report.

16. With respect to agenda item 5 (Consideration of the draft guide on access to credit for micro-, small and medium-sized enterprises), the Commission finalized and adopted the recommendations on access to credit for micro-, small and medium-sized enterprises, which are reproduced in annex V to the present report, and approved in principle the draft commentary to those recommendations.

17. With respect to agenda item 6, the UNCITRAL Colloquium on Climate Change and International Trade Law took place on 12 and 13 July 2023 to consider areas in which international trade law can effectively support the achievement of climate action goals set by the international community, the scope and value of legal harmonization in those areas and the need for international guidance for legislators, policymakers, courts and dispute resolution bodies. The programme of the Colloquium is reproduced in annex VI to the present report.

18. With respect to agenda item 7 (Consideration of the draft guidance text on early dismissal and preliminary determination for inclusion in the UNCITRAL Notes on Organizing Arbitral Proceedings), the Commission finalized and adopted the guidance text on early dismissal and preliminary determination, which is reproduced in annex VII to the present report.

19. With respect to agenda item 8 (Progress reports of working groups), the Commission took note of the progress reports of Working Group II (Dispute Settlement), Working Group III (Investor-State Dispute Settlement Reform), Working Group IV (Electronic Commerce), Working Group V (Insolvency Law) and Working Group VI (Negotiable Multimodal Transport Documents). The Commission expressed its satisfaction with the progress made by those working groups. The work of Working

Group I (Micro-, Small and Medium-sized Enterprises) was considered under agenda item 5.

20. With respect to agenda item 9 (Coordination and cooperation), the Commission took note of the notes by the Secretariat on coordination activities and on international governmental and non-governmental organizations invited to sessions of UNCITRAL and its working groups, as well as the reports by HCCH, UNIDROIT and PCA.

21. With respect to agenda item 10 (Secretariat reports on non-legislative activities), the Commission took note of the notes by the Secretariat concerning non-legislative activities, and, more specifically:

(a) The Commission expressed its gratitude to States and organizations that had contributed to the UNCITRAL trust funds since the Commission's fifty-fifth session, and called upon all States, international organizations and other interested entities to consider or to continue making contributions to those trust funds;

(b) The Commission welcomed the report on the Transparency Registry and expressed its support for the continued operation of the Transparency Registry as a key mechanism for promoting transparency in investor-State arbitration until the end of 2024 (subject to funding);

(c) The Commission also recalled the importance of ensuring a uniform interpretation and application of its texts and reiterated its call for contributions from all legal traditions to its uniform interpretation tools. The Commission noted with interest the progress towards rejuvenation of the Case Law on UNCITRAL Texts (CLOUT) system, and welcomed the signing of new CLOUT Network institutional partnerships;

(d) The Commission also noted with interest the further expansion of engagement with academic partners, geared towards young researchers and practitioners in international trade law, including the UNCITRAL Asia-Pacific Days, the UNCITRAL Latin American and Caribbean Days and the UNCITRAL Days in Africa, and noted that reports on the 2022 editions of the UNCITRAL Days were available on its website; and

(e) The Commission requested the secretariat to facilitate an open and flexible intersessional consultative process among States Members of the United Nations with a view to developing guidelines on streamlining and simplifying the text of future draft omnibus resolutions to be adopted by the General Assembly, and report back to the Commission at its next session.

22. With respect to agenda item 11 (Work programme of the Commission), the Commission:

(a) Confirmed the programme of current legislative activities carried out by its Working Groups II, III, IV, V and VI;

(b) Agreed to refer the draft model law on warehouse receipts developed by the joint UNIDROIT/UNCITRAL Working Group to Working Group I;

(c) Authorized the secretariat to finalize and publish the document entitled "COVID-19 and international trade law instruments: a legal toolkit by the UNCITRAL secretariat";

(d) Requested the secretariat, within the UNCITRAL mandate and in cooperation and collaboration with the secretariat of the United Nations Framework Convention on Climate Change (UNFCCC), UNIDROIT, HCCH and other organizations with relevant expertise, to consult with all States Members of the United Nations, in particular developing countries, with a view to developing a more detailed study on the aspects of international trade law related to voluntary carbon credits;

(e) Asked the secretariat to continue and finalize its work on the preparation of a guidance document on legal issues relating to the use of distributed ledger systems in trade, within existing resources, and in cooperation with other concerned organizations, as appropriate;

(f) Requested the secretariat to continue to implement the project on the stocktaking of developments in dispute resolution in the digital economy and to put forward proposals for possible legislative work with a focus on the topics on the recognition and enforcement of electronic awards and electronic notices of arbitration and their service, and to report on further progress made overall.

23. With respect to agenda item 11 (Work programme of the Commission), under the subtopic of methods of work, the Commission:

(a) Requested the secretariat to seek ways to continue the livestreaming of UNCITRAL sessions within the existing resources of the secretariat;

(b) Confirmed that Working Group III, or any other working group when the need arose, could continue to use the final meetings of its sessions for substantive deliberations and adopt the report of the session by means of a written procedure;

(c) Agreed that each working group should decide how and when informal meetings of the working group would be organized by the secretariat in between its sessions.

24. With respect to agenda item 12 (Date and place of future meetings), the Commission approved the holding of its fifty-seventh session in New York from 24 June to 12 July 2024 and the schedule for working group sessions to be held in the second half of 2023 and first half of 2024.

IV. Consideration of texts prepared in the context of investor-State dispute settlement reform

A. Introduction

25. The Committee of the Whole recalled that the Commission, at its fiftieth session, in 2017, had entrusted Working Group III with a broad mandate to work on the possible reform of investor-State dispute settlement.[2] It was also recalled that, at its fifty-fifth session, in 2022, the Commission had expressed its satisfaction with the progress made by Working Group III and encouraged the Working Group to submit to the Commission for consideration at its fifty-sixth session a code of conduct with commentary and texts on alternative dispute resolution mechanisms.[3]

26. The Committee noted that Working Group III had conducted work during its forty-third and forty-fifth sessions on the draft provisions on mediation and the draft guidelines on investment mediation, both of which aimed to encourage the use of mediation as a means of resolving investment disputes in a cost-effective manner, while preserving the relationship between the investor and the State (A/CN.9/1124, para. 145). The Committee noted that both texts would address the concerns identified by the Working Group regarding the cost and duration of investor-State dispute settlement proceedings and could improve the efficiency of such proceedings.

27. The Committee further noted that Working Group III had continued its work on a code of conduct from its forty-third session to its forty-fifth session. It was noted that, at its forty-third session, the Working Group had decided to work towards presenting two separate texts to the Commission – a code of conduct for arbitrators for its adoption and a code of conduct for judges for its adoption in principle, which would provide flexibility to revisit any pending issues and make any necessary adjustments once the deliberations on the standing mechanism had progressed (A/CN.9/1124, para. 204). It was further noted that at its forty-fourth and forty-fifth sessions, the Working Group had approved the draft code of conduct for arbitrators in international investment dispute resolution and the draft code of conduct for judges in international investment dispute resolution, both with accompanying commentary, and had requested the

[2] *Official Records of the General Assembly, Seventy-second Session, Supplement No. 17* (A/72/17), para. 264.

[3] Ibid., *Seventy-seventh Session, Supplement No. 17* (A/77/17), paras. 179 and 194 (c).

secretariat to present them to the Commission for its consideration (A/CN.9/1130, para. 117, and A/CN.9/1131, para. 86).

28. At the present session, the Commission had before it the following documents: (a) draft provisions on mediation (A/CN.9/1150); (b) draft UNCITRAL guidelines on investment mediation (A/CN.9/1151); (c) the draft code of conduct for arbitrators in international investment dispute resolution and commentary (A/CN.9/1148); and (d) the draft code of conduct for judges in international investment dispute resolution and commentary (A/CN.9/1149).

29. As decided by the Commission (see para. 13 above), the Committee considered the above-mentioned texts and approved the texts subject to the amendments set out below.

B. Finalization and adoption of the UNCITRAL Model Provisions on Mediation for International Investment Disputes

1. Consideration of the draft provisions on mediation

Draft provision 1

30. It was said that paragraph 6 provided a default rule for instances when the parties had not agreed on the mediation rules or when the mediation rules agreed by the parties did not address when the mediation would commence. Accordingly, it was agreed that the paragraph should be included as the first subparagraph in paragraph 8, making it subject to the applicable mediation rules. It was further observed that paragraph 9 would allow the parties to agree on a date when the mediation would commence, which might differ from that provided for in paragraph 6. It was also clarified that the form requirement of the acceptance of the invitation was already provided for in paragraph 5 and did not need to be addressed in paragraph 6.

Draft provision 2

31. A suggestion that an invitation to engage in mediation should include additional information (such as proposals for the applicable rules, the mediator, the appointing authority or the applicable law) did not receive support, as it was observed that draft provision 2 only addressed the minimum information that would be required in the invitation.

Draft provision 3

32. It was observed that paragraph 2 would not create an obligation on the parties to engage in mediation and that there might be a wide range of means for a party or parties to request the suspension of the other proceeding.

Draft provision 4

33. With regard to the annotation to draft provision 4 (A/CN.9/1150, para. 17), it was observed that views, proposals, admissions or the willingness to settle expressed during the mediation should not be used in other proceedings regardless of whether that was to the detriment of the party who made them. In that context, it was clarified that the annotations were prepared for reference only and would not be published together with the provisions.

Title of the draft provisions

34. After discussion, the Committee agreed that the draft provisions should be called the "UNCITRAL Model Provisions on Mediation for International Investment Disputes".

2. Adoption of the UNCITRAL Model Provisions on Mediation for International Investment Disputes

35. At its 1188th meeting, on 7 July 2023, the Commission adopted by consensus the following decision:

"*The United Nations Commission on International Trade Law*,

"*Recalling* its mandate under General Assembly resolution 2205 (XXI) of 17 December 1966 to further the progressive harmonization and unification of the law of international trade and in that respect to bear in mind the interests of all peoples, in particular those of developing countries, in the extensive development of international trade,

"*Recalling also* its decision at the fiftieth session in July 2017 to entrust Working Group III (Investor-State Dispute Settlement Reform) with a broad mandate to work on the possible reform of investor-State dispute settlement and to develop relevant solutions,[4]

"*Recalling further* its decision at its fifty-fourth session in July 2021 adopting the UNCITRAL Mediation Rules, where the value of mediation was recognized as a method for amicably and effectively settling disputes arising in the context of international commercial relations,[5]

"*Noting* that Working Group III, in carrying out its mandate, had identified the desirability of encouraging the use of mediation for resolving international investment disputes in a cost- and time-efficient manner by preparing draft provisions on mediation,

"*Recognizing* that there are significant benefits to mediation, such as allowing parties to exercise control over the process to reach a self-tailored outcome and preserve their relationship, as well as providing necessary safeguards for due process,

"*Convinced* that a clear legal basis signals the availability of mediation as a means for international investment dispute resolution,

"*Mindful* that Working Group III is continuing to make progress with regard to a number of investor-State dispute settlement reform elements to be recommended to the Commission, which could provide additional means to apply provisions on mediation,

"*Noting* that the preparation of the draft provisions on mediation benefited greatly from consultations with Governments and interested intergovernmental and non-governmental organizations,

"*Expressing its appreciation* to Working Group III for formulating the draft provisions on mediation,

"1. *Adopts* the UNCITRAL Model Provisions on Mediation for International Investment Disputes, as they appear in annex I to the report of the United Nations Commission on International Trade Law on the work of its fifty-sixth session;

"2. *Recommends* that States and other relevant stakeholders involved in the negotiation of international investment instruments consider including the UNCITRAL Model Provisions on Mediation for International Investment Disputes into the respective instrument;

"3. *Requests* the Secretary-General to publish the UNCITRAL Model Provisions on Mediation for International Investment Disputes, including electronically, in the six official languages of the United Nations, and to disseminate them broadly to Governments and other interested bodies."

---

[4] A/72/17, para. 264.

[5] *Official Records of the General Assembly, Seventy-sixth Session, Supplement No. 17* (A/76/17), para. 101.

C. Finalization and adoption of the UNCITRAL Guidelines on Mediation for International Investment Disputes

1. Consideration of the draft UNCITRAL guidelines on investment mediation

Paragraph 2

36. The Committee of the Whole agreed to delete the words "international investment" in the second sentence of paragraph 2 and to add at the end of that paragraph the following sentence: "Therefore, mediation can also be an effective tool to resolve international investment disputes."

Paragraph 15

37. While a suggestion was made to add "upon the request of the respective party" in the second sentence of paragraph 15, it was generally felt that the addition was not necessary as the word "assist" implied that it was upon the request of a party.

Paragraph 26

38. The Committee agreed that the last sentence of paragraph 26 should be revised as follows: "Information about the authority of the participants in the mediation to settle should be shared with the mediator and the other parties at an early stage of the mediation."

Title of the draft guidelines

39. The Committee agreed that the phrase "investment mediation" in the draft guidelines should be replaced with the phrase "mediation for international investment disputes" for clarity (for example, paragraphs 1, 37 and 38, as well as the heading of section J of the draft guidelines). Accordingly, the Committee also agreed that the draft guidelines should be called the "UNCITRAL Guidelines on Mediation for International Investment Disputes".

2. Adoption of the UNCITRAL Guidelines on Mediation for International Investment Disputes

40. At its 1188th meeting, on 7 July 2023, the Commission adopted by consensus the following decision:

"*The United Nations Commission on International Trade Law*,

"*Recalling* its mandate under General Assembly resolution 2205 (XXI) of 17 December 1966 to further the progressive harmonization and unification of the law of international trade and in that respect to bear in mind the interests of all peoples, in particular those of developing countries, in the extensive development of international trade,

"*Recalling also* its decision at the fiftieth session in July 2017 to entrust Working Group III (Investor-State Dispute Settlement Reform) with a broad mandate to work on the possible reform of investor-State dispute settlement and to develop relevant solutions,

"*Recalling further* its decision at the fifty-fourth session in July 2021 adopting the UNCITRAL Mediation Rules, where the value of mediation was recognized as a method for amicably and effectively settling disputes arising in the context of international commercial relations,[6]

"*Noting* that Working Group III, in carrying out its mandate, had identified the desirability of encouraging the use of mediation for resolving international investment disputes in a cost- and time-efficient manner,

[6] Ibid., para. 101.

"*Recognizing* that there are significant benefits to mediation, such as allowing parties to exercise control over the process to reach a self-tailored outcome and preserve their relationship, as well as providing necessary safeguards for due process,

"*Noting* that the preparations of the draft UNCITRAL guidelines on investment mediation benefited greatly from consultations with Governments and interested intergovernmental and non-governmental organizations,

"*Expressing its appreciation* to Working Group III for formulating the draft UNCITRAL guidelines on investment mediation,

"1. *Adopts* the UNCITRAL Guidelines on Mediation for International Investment Disputes consisting of the text contained in document A/CN.9/1151, with amendments as reflected in the report of the United Nations Commission on International Trade Law on the work of its fifty-sixth session,[7] and authorizes the secretariat to finalize the text of the Guidelines pursuant to the decisions of the Commission at that session;[8]

"2. *Recommends* the use of the UNCITRAL Guidelines on Mediation for International Investment Disputes, by States, investors, mediators, interested institutions and other relevant stakeholders to foster a better understanding of mediation with regard to resolution of international investment disputes;

"3. *Requests* the Secretary-General to publish the UNCITRAL Guidelines on Mediation for International Investment Disputes, including electronically, in the six official languages of the United Nations, and to disseminate it broadly to Governments and other interested bodies."

D. Finalization and adoption of the UNCITRAL Code of Conduct for Arbitrators in International Investment Dispute Resolution and adoption in principle of the UNCITRAL Code of Conduct for Judges in International Investment Dispute Resolution, both with accompanying commentary

1. Consideration of the draft code of conduct for arbitrators in international investment dispute resolution and commentary

Article 1

41. With regard to article 1 of the draft code of conduct for arbitrators in international investment dispute resolution, the Committee of the Whole agreed to insert an additional subparagraph after subparagraph (e) to read as follows: "'Applicable rules' means the applicable arbitration rules and any law applicable to the IID proceeding."

42. With respect to paragraph 6 of the draft commentary, the Committee agreed to revise the first sentence as follows: "... refers to an agreement made with regard to an investment that a foreign investor makes in the territory of a State or a State of a REIO (...).". While it was said that the last sentence might be intrusive of the sovereignty of States, particularly with regard to disputes with domestic investors, the Committee agreed to add the word "also" before the words "to apply", which would highlight that the second sentence of article 2, paragraph 1, provided an additional means for the disputing parties to apply the Code without necessarily recommending that they do so.

43. The Committee further agreed to delete the quotation marks in paragraph 7 of the draft commentary as the terms were not defined in the draft code and to place the

[7] *Official Records of the General Assembly, Seventy-eighth Session, Supplement No. 17* (A/78/17), paras. 36–40.

[8] The text of the Guidelines as finalized by the secretariat can be found in annex II to the present report.

words "to resolve an IID" in the first sentence of paragraph 8 of the draft commentary at the end of that sentence to better reflect the definition in article 1, paragraph (c).

Article 2

44. With regard to article 2, paragraph 2, of the draft code, proposals to delete the first sentence and retain only the second sentence as well as to include language allowing the disputing parties to vary the rule in the second sentence did not receive support.

45. While suggestions were made that the commentary could list the different means of implementing the code and that users should be encouraged to apply the code in a harmonized and uniform fashion, it was widely felt that those issues would be better addressed in the decision adopting the code (see para. 90 below). This was largely due to the fact that there could be several ways of implementing the code and that it would be difficult to address all such circumstances in the commentary in sufficient detail.

46. With respect to the draft commentary, it was suggested that paragraph 15 should be revised so that it addressed a situation where the code would not have been incorporated into the instrument of consent but was made applicable by other means (for example, by agreement of the disputing parties or incorporation into the applicable arbitration rules). In that regard, it was observed that if the code were incorporated into the instrument of consent (for example, an investment treaty), the relationship between the code and any provision in that treaty addressing the conduct of arbitrators would usually be set forth in the treaty itself. Accordingly, it was suggested that paragraphs 15 to 18 of the draft commentary should be revised to better clarify the relationship between the articles in the code and provisions in the instrument of consent.

47. Doubts were expressed about paragraph 16 of the draft commentary being overly prescriptive and possibly limiting the ways the code could be implemented, including through a multilateral instrument. The meaning of the instrument of consent being "silent" or providing a "lenient" or "stricter" obligation as well as the person that would be making such a determination were questioned. On the other hand, it was said that the paragraph provided useful guidance on the complementary nature of the code. It was observed that, while examples contained in that paragraph as well as in paragraph 18 of the draft commentary provided useful guidance, they could cause confusion and that providing a more general explanation of the meaning of the words "complement" and "incompatibility" without specific examples could make the text clearer.

48. It was suggested that paragraph 17 of the draft commentary could be clarified to better explain the meaning of "incompatibility", and that the last two sentences of paragraph 18 of the draft commentary should be deleted.

49. After discussion, the Committee agreed to:

(a) Revise the second sentence of paragraph 13 of the draft commentary to read as follows: "However, the obligations in article 4, paragraphs 2 to 4, as well as article 8, paragraphs 1 and 2, survive the proceeding. In other words, these obligations apply to individuals who served as a member of an arbitral tribunal or an ICSID ad hoc committee ('former Arbitrator').";

(b) Revise paragraphs 15 to 18 as follows:

> "15. The application of article 2, paragraph 2, will largely depend on how the Code is made applicable, including by any rule in the instrument of consent addressing the relationship between the instrument of consent and the Code.
>
> "16. Where the instrument of consent contains provisions on the conduct of an Arbitrator, a Candidate or a former Arbitrator, and the Code is also otherwise made applicable, paragraph 2 in the Code applies. Pursuant to

the first sentence of paragraph 2, if the relevant provisions in the instrument of consent and in the Code are not incompatible, the provisions of the instrument of consent are complemented by the provisions of the Code. In that case, an Arbitrator, a Candidate or a former Arbitrator is expected to comply with the obligations in the instrument of consent as well as in the Code. However, where the relevant provisions in the instrument of consent and in the Code are incompatible, for example, when an Arbitrator, a Candidate or a former Arbitrator cannot comply with both, then pursuant to the second sentence of paragraph 2, the provisions in the instrument of consent would prevail. Certain articles of the Code reflect this general principle (see the phrase 'unless permitted by the instrument of consent' in articles 7 and 8)."

Article 3

50. With respect to the draft commentary, the Committee agreed to:

(a) Simplify paragraph 20 to read as follows: "Existing standards prepared by international bodies, such as the 2014 International Bar Association (IBA) Guidelines on Conflicts of Interest in International Arbitration (the "IBA Guidelines"), may provide useful guidance in this regard.";

(b) Replace the words "a member of an arbitral tribunal" in the first sentence of paragraph 21 with the words "an Arbitrator";

(c) Delete the word "written" before the word "submission" in the second sentence of paragraph 24; and

(d) Revise the second and third sentences of paragraph 28 as follows: "... and whether the advancement was realized is irrelevant. Even if the advantage gained or sought was insignificant ...".

Article 4

51. With regard to article 4 of the draft code, a suggestion was made that the code should be expanded to limit a former legal representative or a former expert witness from acting as an Arbitrator for a certain period of time after he or she ceased to exercise such functions similar to that provided for in article 4, paragraphs 2 to 4. In response, it was pointed out that the code aimed to address the conduct of arbitrators and former arbitrators and not that of legal representatives or expert witnesses. It was further mentioned that such individuals would in any case be bound by the independence and impartiality obligation in article 3 and disclosure obligations in article 11 if he or she were to function as an Arbitrator. It was also mentioned that article 4, paragraph 1, would prohibit such individuals from functioning concurrently as an Arbitrator requiring them to resign as a legal representative or an expert witness.

52. Another suggestion was to clarify in paragraphs 2 to 4 of article 4 that the "disputing parties" referred to the parties to the proceeding which the former Arbitrator had adjudicated. However, it was agreed that this would be better explained in the commentary than in the article itself.

53. With respect to paragraph 32 of the draft commentary, the Committee agreed to delete the phrase ", which may vary depending on when the IID proceeding is concluded" in the last sentence. The Committee further agreed that the references to paragraph 1 of article 4 of the code in the first sentences of paragraphs 34, 36, 37 and 38 should be revised, respectively, to "the limitations in article 4", "paragraphs 1 and 2", "paragraphs 1 and 3", and "paragraphs 1 and 4".

54. With respect to paragraph 38 of the draft commentary, a suggestion was made to include an additional example as follows: "For example, an Arbitrator interpreting a treaty provision in order to analyse the context or object and purpose of the treaty in relation to another treaty provision may not concurrently act as a legal

representative in another proceeding addressing either treaty provision." That suggestion did not receive support.

55. The Committee agreed to split paragraph 39 of the draft commentary into two paragraphs, with the first two sentences as the first paragraph. It was further agreed that the second paragraph would read as follows: "For paragraph 1, the phrase 'disputing parties' refers to the parties to the proceeding that the Arbitrator is adjudicating (in the case where the Arbitrator has been appointed and is requesting to act as a legal representative or an expert witness in the circumstances identified) or is expected to adjudicate (in the case where a Candidate wishes to continue to work as a legal representative or an expert witness in the circumstances identified). For paragraphs 2 to 4, the same phrase refers to the parties to the proceeding that the former Arbitrator had adjudicated and not the parties to the proceeding in which the former Arbitrator is expected to act or is acting as a legal representative or an expert witness."

56. Diverging views were expressed on paragraph 40 of the draft commentary which addressed a problem that could arise in practice when a former Arbitrator sought to obtain the agreement of the disputing parties. One view was that the general rule should be to require the "express" agreement of the disputing parties. It was further mentioned that the circumstances in which the agreement of the disputing party could be implied under paragraph 40 were uncertain, particularly as it would be based on a subjective assessment by the former Arbitrator on whether "reasonable" steps were taken and whether a "reasonable" period of time had lapsed. It was suggested that any deeming provision to that effect should be contained in the code itself and not merely in the commentary.

57. Another view was that paragraph 40 addressed a problem that could arise in practice and provided useful guidance for situations where a former Arbitrator sought to obtain the agreement of the disputing parties but it would not be possible for a disputing party to respond to the request to waive the requirements in paragraphs 2 to 4 of article 4 of the code (for example, if the individual had passed away or a corporate entity had dissolved). It was further pointed out that if the former Arbitrator had made sufficient effort to obtain the waiver from the disputing party, the former Arbitrator should be able to infer that the disputing party did not object to the waiver. However, views were also expressed that a mere failure to respond should not be deemed a waiver and that the circumstances should be limited to where it was "impossible" for that party to respond.

58. It was mentioned that a similar situation could arise in the context of article 8, paragraph 1, of the draft code as the obligation of confidentiality survived the international investment dispute proceeding and the former Arbitrator might need to seek the permission from the disputing parties, for example, to disclose any information concerning the international investment dispute proceeding.

59. It was suggested that the commentary to article 4 should state that if a disputing party objected to the request by an Arbitrator or a former Arbitrator to vary or waive the obligations in article 4, that would mean that there was no agreement by the disputing parties and the Arbitrator or the former Arbitrator should not accept the role as a legal representative or an expert witness. However, it was pointed out that the inclusion of such text in the commentary might unduly oblige the disputing party to "object", whereas it should be possible for that disputing party to not agree by simply remaining silent.

60. After discussion, the Committee agreed to revise paragraph 40 of the draft commentary as follows: "In paragraphs 2 to 4, the disputing parties are presumed to be capable of responding and are expected to respond to a proposal to vary or waive the requirements specified therein. However, there may be instances where it is impossible for a disputing party to respond, for example, if the disputing party has passed away or is under some other incapacity, or if it has ceased to exist in the case of a corporate entity. In such cases, the former Arbitrator must exercise reasonable diligence to identify if there is a person or entity that is legally authorized to act on

that disputing party's behalf. If no such person or entity can be identified, it can be understood that the former Arbitrator, in those limited circumstances, has obtained the agreement of the disputing parties, if the remaining disputing party or parties provide its/their agreement."

61. The Committee also agreed that paragraph 41 of the draft commentary should be modified as follows: "..., would assist the Arbitrator in complying with article 4 and provide the disputing parties the opportunity to share their views in advance of the Arbitrator taking on the concurrent appointment (see art. 12, para 3, and paras. 44 and 91 below).

Article 6

62. With respect to article 6 (c) of the draft code, a suggestion was made to add the words "unless otherwise provided for in the applicable rules" reflecting paragraph 49 of the draft commentary. However, it was said that in existing arbitration rules, the circumstances in which decision-making functions could be delegated were limited to specific issues and subject to strict conditions. It was further mentioned that such rules did not necessarily address the delegation of decision-making, but rather the authority of the presiding arbitrator to take certain decisions. Lastly, it was mentioned that the inclusion of the additional words might unduly broaden the exception and mitigate the intended signalling of that subparagraph that decision-making functions should not be delegated, particularly to Assistants.

63. After discussion, the Committee agreed to retain article 6 (c) in its current form and to revise paragraph 49 of the draft commentary to read as follows: "The prohibition in subparagraph (c) is without prejudice to provisions in the applicable arbitration rules, which give decision-making authority on certain issues and under certain conditions to the presiding Arbitrator."

64. A suggestion to indicate in paragraph 48 of the draft commentary that an Assistant should be prohibited from drafting "substantive" parts of decisions or awards (for example, pertaining to the settlement of the dispute or the merits of the case) did not receive support.

Article 7

65. With respect to article 7, paragraph 1, and article 8, paragraph 1, of the draft code, it was observed that the use of the definite article "the" before the words "agreement of the disputing parties" assumed that there was an existing agreement by the parties. Accordingly, the Committee agreed to revise paragraph 1 of article 7 as follows: "Unless permitted by the instrument of consent, the applicable rules, agreement of the disputing parties or paragraph 2, ex parte communication is prohibited" (see also para. 68 below).

66. With respect to the draft commentary, the Committee agreed to delete the second sentence of paragraph 52 (see para. 41 above) and to end the last sentence of paragraph 55 after the words "issues of jurisdiction or the merits".

Article 8

67. With respect to article 8 of the draft code, a number of suggestions were made. One was that the obligations in paragraphs 4 and 5 should apply also to a former Arbitrator, similar to the obligations in paragraphs 1 and 2. Another was that the text of paragraph 4 should clarify the meaning of a decision being "publicly available" along the lines found in paragraph 61 of the draft commentary. While concerns were expressed that the inclusion of such language could make it burdensome for an Arbitrator to make the necessary verification, it was said that paragraph 4 applied only to decisions rendered in the proceeding which the Arbitrator was adjudicating and not to other decisions referred to in that proceeding. There was general support for the additional text.

68. After discussion, the Committee agreed to revise article 8 as follows:

“Article 8
“Confidentiality

“1. Unless permitted by the instrument of consent, the applicable rules or agreement of the disputing parties, a Candidate, an Arbitrator, or a former Arbitrator shall not:

“(a) Disclose or use any information concerning, or acquired in connection with, the IID proceeding; or

“(b) Disclose any draft decision in the IID proceeding.

“2. An Arbitrator or a former Arbitrator shall not disclose the contents of the deliberations in the IID proceeding.

“3. An Arbitrator or a former Arbitrator may comment on a decision rendered in the IID proceeding only if it was made publicly available in accordance with the instrument of consent or the applicable rules.

“4. Notwithstanding paragraph 3, an Arbitrator or a former Arbitrator shall not comment on a decision while the IID proceeding is pending or the decision is subject to a post-award remedy or review.

“5. The obligations in this article shall not apply to the extent that a Candidate, an Arbitrator, or a former Arbitrator is legally compelled to disclose the information in a court or other competent body or needs to disclose such information to protect or pursue his or her legal rights or in relation to legal proceedings before a court or other competent body.”

69. With respect to the draft commentary to article 8, the Committee agreed to:

(a) Clarify in paragraphs 57 and 61, and where necessary, that the phrase “the IID proceeding” in article 8 referred to the IID proceeding in which the individual was currently functioning as an Arbitrator or to the IID proceeding in which a former Arbitrator had served as one;

(b) Place the second sentence of paragraph 58 at the end of that paragraph;

(c) Merge the first two sentences of paragraph 61 and retain the last sentence; and

(d) Make any consequential changes as a result of the revisions to article 8 (see para. 68 above).

Article 9

70. With respect to the draft commentary to article 9, the Committee agreed to:

(a) Revise the first sentence of paragraph 66 as follows: “Paragraph 1 provides that the fees and expenses shall be reasonable and in accordance with the instrument of consent or the applicable rules”; and

(b) Revise the second sentence of paragraph 70 as follows: “This is intended to minimize the likelihood of disputes ...”.

Article 10

71. With regard to the draft commentary to article 10, a suggestion was made to include an additional sentence at the end of paragraph 71, to read as follows: “Communications between an Arbitrator and disputing parties regarding a proposed Assistant should be in accordance with article 7 on ex parte communication”. Another suggestion was to replace the phrase “in accordance with” with the phrase “consistent with” in paragraphs 74 and 75 of the draft commentary, as the code was not intended to apply directly to Assistants. Those suggestions did not receive support as all communication between an Arbitrator and the disputing parties would be subject to

article 7 of the draft code and because the phrase “in accordance with” was used in the article itself.

72. With regard to the second sentence of paragraph 72 of the draft commentary, the Committee agreed to align it more closely with paragraph 48 to read as follows: “When an Assistant is tasked with preparing portions of preliminary drafts of decisions or awards ...”.

Article 11

73. With regard to article 11 of the draft code, suggestions to delete paragraph 7 and to replace the phrase “any other IID or related proceeding” in paragraph 2 (e) with “any other proceeding” did not receive support.

74. After discussion (see para. 81 below), the Committee agreed to insert a new paragraph after paragraph 5 as follows: “If a Candidate or an Arbitrator is bound by confidentiality obligations and cannot disclose all of the required circumstances or information in this article, he or she shall make the disclosure to the extent possible. If a Candidate or an Arbitrator is unable to disclose circumstances that are likely to give rise to justifiable doubts as to his or her independence or impartiality, he or she shall not accept the appointment or shall resign or recuse himself or herself from the IID proceeding.”

75. With respect to the draft commentary to article 11, the Committee first considered the reformulation of paragraphs 78. While some preference was expressed for retaining the current formulation, it was generally felt that the broad disclosure obligation required under article 11 was equally reflected in the reformulated text. With respect to that text, suggestions were made to refer to a reasonable “third” person and to delete the words “reasonable” and to insert “reasonably” before the words “reach the conclusion” in the second sentence. With regard to the new paragraph 78bis, a suggestion was made to delete the words “in the eyes of a disputing party” and add at the end the words “in the particular case”. After discussion, the Committee decided to replace the current paragraph 78 with the reformulated text and to insert the text in paragraph 78bis at the end of paragraph 94.

76. The Committee further agreed to revise the second sentence of paragraph 79 of the draft commentary as follows: “For example, the 2014 IBA Guidelines may provide ...” (see para. 50 above).

77. With regard to paragraph 90 of the draft commentary, the view was expressed that the reference to article 4 at the end of that paragraph was not necessary as other articles of the code would be relevant as well, for example, article 3. Another view was that it would be necessary to clarify when the circumstances would be prohibited under article 4 or at least add the words “where relevant” to clarify the meaning. The Committee decided to retain paragraph 90 without any change.

78. The Committee agreed to revise paragraph 91 of the draft commentary as follows: “Subparagraph (c) requires a Candidate or an Arbitrator to inform the disputing parties prior to taking on a new role allowing the disputing parties to ask questions and to share any views that they may have that a Candidate or an Arbitrator acting concurrently as a legal representative or an expert witness in any other IID or related proceeding would violate articles 3 or 4 of the Code.”

79. With respect to the second sentence of paragraph 96 of the draft commentary, the Committee agreed to add “the applicable rules,” after “depend on”.

80. A number of suggestions were made with respect to paragraph 99 of the draft commentary. One was that its content should be formulated as a rule in the code, which received support (see para. 74 above). Another was that the sources of confidentiality might vary and not be limited to article 8 of the code. Yet another suggestion was to elaborate that a Candidate would need to indicate all paragraphs or subparagraphs of article 11 to which the information subject to confidentiality related.

81. After discussion, the Committee agreed to revise paragraph 99 of the draft commentary as follows: "In accordance with paragraph 6, when a Candidate or an Arbitrator is bound by confidentiality obligations and is not in a position to disclose all of the required circumstances or information, he or she should disclose as much as possible to allow an assessment of his or her impartiality and independence by the disputing parties. For example, with regard to the list of proceedings in subparagraph (c) (see para. 89 above), a Candidate could redact certain information, disclose the region where the claimant or the respondent is located, the relevant industry or sector, the applicable rules, and indicate that he or she is bound by a confidentiality obligation and that the information subject to confidentiality relates to subparagraph 2 (c). However, if a Candidate is unable to disclose circumstances that are likely to give rise to justifiable doubts to his independence and impartiality, he or she should decline the appointment in accordance with paragraph 6."

Article 12

82. The Committee agreed to revise article 12, paragraph 1, of the draft code as follows: "An Arbitrator, a former Arbitrator and a Candidate shall comply with the Code."

83. With respect to paragraph 100 of the draft commentary, the Committee confirmed that the first sentence illustrated the best practice of signing a declaration upon appointment and agreed to add in the second sentence a reference to article 6 (b) of the code.

2. Consideration of the draft code of conduct for judges in international investment dispute resolution and commentary

84. At the outset, views were expressed that it would be premature to consider or finalize the draft code of conduct for judges for presentation to the Commission for its adoption in principle, as Working Group III had not decided on the possible establishment of a standing mechanism to resolve investment disputes, to which the code could apply. It was stated that the desirability of establishing such a standing mechanism was not shared by all and that a number of aspects relating to the establishment were yet to be discussed by the Working Group. A concern was expressed regarding the significant number of placeholders in the text of the code as well as blanket references to yet non-existing instruments. A doubt was also expressed about adopting the code in principle as it might need to be revised in the future given any decision by the Working Group.

85. In response, it was pointed out that Working Group III was in the process of considering the possible establishment of a standing mechanism with the code of conduct for judges being an element of it. It was also pointed out that the Working Group had agreed to develop the codes of conduct for arbitrators and for judges in parallel and to present reform elements on a rolling basis to the Commission rather than waiting for all of the elements to be finalized. It was also mentioned that some existing investment treaties contained references to the possible establishment of a standing mechanism and a code of conduct for judges. It was recalled that it was in that context that Working Group III recommended that the code of conduct for judges be adopted in principle, unlike the code of conduct for arbitrators, which was recommended for adoption by the Commission.

86. After discussion, the Committee agreed to review the text of the draft code for judges in international investment dispute resolution and its draft commentary, which would be without prejudice to the views of States on the desirability of establishing a standing mechanism to resolve investment disputes as well as any future determination by the Working Group with respect to whether it would recommend this reform element to the Commission.

(a) Draft code of conduct

87. The Committee agreed to revise article 1 (a) of the draft code as follows: "'Judge' means a person who is a member of a standing mechanism". The Committee further agreed to delete the commas in the second sentence of article 4, paragraph 1, to ensure that the limitation in that sentence only relates to occupations incompatible with the obligation of independence and impartiality or with the demands of the terms of office.

88. A suggestion to impose limitations on judges similar to those found in article 4, paragraphs 2 to 4, of the draft code of conduct for arbitrators in international investment dispute resolution did not receive support.

(b) Draft commentary

89. With respect to the commentary to the Code, the Committee agreed to:

(a) Delete the phrase "to adjudicate international investment disputes" in paragraph 1, so as not to pre-determine the scope of jurisdiction of a standing mechanism;

(b) Delete the term "written" in the second sentence of paragraph 11;

(c) Revise the second and third sentences of paragraph 15 as follows: "... and whether the advancement was realized is irrelevant. Even if the advantage gained or sought was insignificant ...";

(d) Delete the comma in the first sentence of paragraph 19;

(e) Revise paragraph 24 to read as follows: "The specific duties of a Judge under article 5 are to be found under the terms of office or in the rules of the standing mechanism.";

(f) Revise paragraph 26 as follows: "... is without prejudice to rules of the standing mechanism, for example, one which gives decision-making authority on certain issues and under certain conditions to the Judge who functions as the president of the standing mechanism";

(g) Restructure paragraph 28 so that the first sentence would be combined with paragraph 29, the second sentence would be placed after paragraph 32 (as an exception to the general rule) and the third sentence would be deleted (leaving flexibility to the rules of the standing mechanism);

(h) Revise the second sentence of paragraph 35 as follows: "Doubts are justifiable if a reasonable person, having knowledge of the relevant facts and circumstances, would reach the conclusion that there is a likelihood that a Candidate or a Judge may be influenced by factors other than the merits of the case as presented by the disputing parties in reaching his or her decision.";

(i) Insert the following at the end of paragraph 47: "A Candidate or a Judge shall err in favour of disclosure in accordance with paragraph 7 and should therefore ensure that his or her disclosure includes circumstances that may, in the eyes of a disputing party, give rise to doubts as to his or her impartiality or independence.";

(j) Revise paragraph 51 as follows: "When a Candidate or a Judge is bound by confidentiality obligations and is not in a position to disclose all of the required circumstances or information in article 9, he or she should inform the appointing authority accordingly and make the disclosure to the extent possible to allow an assessment of his or her impartiality and independence. For example, with regard to the list of proceedings in paragraph 2, a Candidate could redact certain information, disclose the region where the parties are located, the relevant industry or sector, the applicable rules, and indicate that he or she is bound by a confidentiality obligation and that the information subject to confidentiality relates to paragraph 2."

3. Adoption of the UNCITRAL Code of Conduct for Arbitrators in International Investment Dispute Resolution and adoption in principle of the UNCITRAL Code of Conduct for Judges in International Investment Dispute Resolution, both with accompanying commentary

90. At its 1188th meeting, on 7 July 2023, the Commission adopted by consensus the following decision:

"*The United Nations Commission on International Trade Law*,

"*Recalling* its mandate under General Assembly resolution 2205 (XXI) of 17 December 1966 to further the progressive harmonization and unification of the law of international trade and in that respect to bear in mind the interests of all peoples, in particular those of developing countries, in the extensive development of international trade,

"*Recalling also* its decision at the fiftieth session in July 2017 to entrust Working Group III (Investor-State Dispute Settlement Reform) with a broad mandate to work on the possible reform of investor-State dispute settlement and to develop relevant solutions,[9]

"*Noting* that Working Group III had identified the desirability of developing a set of ethical standards for adjudicators responsible for resolving international investment disputes in light of concerns identified by the Working Group about the perceived or apparent lack of independence and impartiality of some adjudicators, which often gave rise to criticism about the legitimacy of the investor-State dispute settlement system,

"*Convinced* that establishing and promulgating clear obligations on adjudicators with regard to, among others, independence and impartiality, limitation on multiple roles, ex parte communication, confidentiality and disclosure would be an appropriate response to the identified concerns,

"*Convinced also* that the development of uniform standards that would apply to arbitrators involved in the resolution of international investment disputes would be highly desirable,

"*Mindful* that Working Group III is continuing to consider whether to recommend a number of investor-State dispute settlement reform elements to the Commission, including the possible establishment of a standing mechanism to resolve international investment disputes and that a code of conduct for members of such a standing mechanism (referred to as 'judges') could form part of the rules governing that mechanism,

"*Mindful also* that Working Group III is considering the development of a multilateral instrument to implement the investor-State dispute settlement reform elements, which could provide additional means to apply the codes of conduct,

"*Noting* that the preparation of the codes of conduct and the accompanying commentary, benefited greatly from consultations with Governments and interested intergovernmental and non-governmental organizations, and in particular, that the draft versions of the codes of conduct were prepared jointly by the secretariats of the International Centre for Settlement of Investment Disputes and the Commission,

"*Expressing its appreciation* to Working Group III for formulating the draft code of conduct for arbitrators in international investment dispute resolution and accompanying commentary as well as the draft code of conduct for judges in international investment dispute resolution and accompanying commentary,

"1. *Adopts* the UNCITRAL Code of Conduct for Arbitrators in International Investment Dispute Resolution (the 'UNCITRAL Code of Conduct for Arbitrators'), as it appears in annex III to the report of the United Nations Commission on

[9] A/72/17, para. 264.

International Trade Law on the work of its fifty-sixth session,[10] as well as the accompanying commentary;

"2. *Adopts in principle* the UNCITRAL Code of Conduct for Judges in International Investment Dispute Resolution (the 'UNCITRAL Code of Conduct for Judges'), as it appears in annex IV to the report of the United Nations Commission on International Trade Law on the work of its fifty-sixth session,[11] as well as the accompanying commentary;

"3. *Recommends* the use of the UNCITRAL Code of Conduct for Arbitrators by arbitrators, former arbitrators, candidates, disputing parties and administering institutions, with regard to international investment disputes;

"4. *Also recommends* the use of the UNCITRAL Code of Conduct for Judges by standing mechanisms, where relevant;

"5. *Further recommends* that States and other relevant stakeholders involved in the negotiation of international investment instruments and the enactment of legislation governing foreign investments make reference to the UNCITRAL Code of Conduct for Arbitrators and the UNCITRAL Code of Conduct for Judges, as appropriate;

"6. *Requests* the Secretary-General to publish the UNCITRAL Code of Conduct for Arbitrators and commentary and the UNCITRAL Code of Conduct for Judges and commentary, including electronically, in the six official languages of the United Nations, and to make all efforts to ensure that the codes and their commentary become generally known and available by disseminating them broadly to Governments and other interested bodies."

V. Consideration of the draft guide on access to credit for micro-, small and medium-sized enterprises

A. Introduction

91. The Commission recalled the decision taken at its fifty-second session, in 2019, to entrust Working Group I with work aimed at facilitating access to credit for micro-, small and medium-sized enterprises (MSMEs), which would draw on the relevant recommendations and guidance contained in the UNCITRAL Model Law on Secured Transactions, as appropriate.[12] It further recalled that such work would strengthen and complete the mandate given to the Working Group by the Commission at its forty-sixth session, in 2013, to work on reducing legal obstacles faced by MSMEs throughout their life cycles, in particular in developing economies.[13]

92. The Commission considered the text of the draft guide on access to credit for micro-, small and medium-sized enterprises as contained in document A/CN.9/1156. Several delegations noted instances where choice of terminology could be refined, and requested the secretariat to review and revise all language versions accordingly. The Commission approved changes to the draft guide as set out below. Recommendations and paragraphs of the draft commentary not referred to below were adopted as drafted.

[10] A/78/17.

[11] Ibid.

[12] *Official Records of the General Assembly, Seventy-fourth Session, Supplement No. 17* (A/74/17), para. 192 (a).

[13] Ibid., *Sixty-eighth Session, Supplement No. 17* (A/68/17), paras. 316–322.

B. Consideration of the draft recommendations

Recommendation 5

93. The Commission adopted subparagraph (b)(iv) as follows: "(iv) Enable creditors to determine the priority of their security rights when entering into the transaction by referring to the registry." It was noted that the Commission would review and discuss the related draft commentary so as to clarify that the reference to the registry was intended to indicate priority in time of the security right in respect of other registered security rights.

94. The Commission adopted subparagraph (c) as follows:

> "The secured transactions regime should apply to all transactions in which movable assets are provided as collateral to secure payment or other performance of an obligation, including those in which the creditor retains title to an asset or title to an asset is transferred to the creditor in order to secure an obligation and regardless of whether the parties have denominated the creditor's right as a security right."

95. A proposal to include the phrase "regardless of the type of asset, the status of the grantor or secured creditor, or the nature of the secured obligation" at the end of subparagraph (c) did not receive sufficient support.

96. The view was expressed that subparagraph (b)(ii) did not specify the relevant mechanisms for creating security right in future assets. In response, it was explained that the possibility of creating a security right in future assets was an essential element for the work of UNCITRAL in the field of security rights and detailed explanations could be found in UNCITRAL texts on secured transactions (e.g. United Nations Convention on the Assignment of Receivables in International Trade, New York, 2001, and UNCITRAL Legislative Guide on Secured Transactions, 2007, introduction, para. 62, and chap. II, paras. 51–55).

Recommendation 6

97. The Commission adopted recommendation 6 as follows:

> "The law should provide for a secured transactions regime with respect to immovable assets which allows:
>
> "(a) The creation of security rights over all types of immovable assets by all types of persons to secure all types of obligations;
>
> "(b) The determination of the priority of the secured creditor's rights when entering into the transaction; and
>
> "(c) The realization of security rights over immovable assets."

98. A suggestion for subparagraph (b) to refer to the simple and economically efficient realization of security rights over immovable assets did not receive sufficient support because the UNCITRAL texts in the area of security interests, in particular the UNCITRAL Model Law on Secured Transactions[14] referred to simple and economically efficient means for the realization of security rights to encourage States to allow also out-of-court enforcement of security rights over moveable property. It was noted that, in respect of immovable assets, this might not be possible in most jurisdictions. A suggestion for the draft recommendation to refer to specific types of sources of credit (e.g. leasing and collective credit arrangements) did not receive support.

[14] United Nations publication, Sales No. E.17.V.1.

Recommendation 7

99. The Commission adopted recommendation 7 as follows:

"To help ensure that guarantors and financers of MSMEs are aware of their rights and obligations, the law should:

"(a) Require the terms and conditions of the guarantee to be clear, understandable and legible; and

"(b) Identify both the formalities and content requirements necessary to make a guarantee effective."

Recommendation 8

100. The Commission adopted recommendation 8 as follows:

"To enable financers to more accurately assess the creditworthiness of MSMEs who are potential borrowers, the law should:

"(a) Establish a legal and regulatory framework for the creation and operation of public or private commercial credit reporting systems; and

"(b) Specify the nature and scope of reporting obligations with respect to such systems."

Recommendation 9

101. A concern was expressed regarding the reference to "existing international standards" on the basis that the term "standard" might be interpreted as being legally binding in some jurisdictions. In response, it was explained that the title of instruments cited by way of example in the draft recommendation made it clear that these instruments were only legislative guides. It was recalled that the term "standard" had been used in General Assembly resolutions concerning the work of UNCITRAL[15] to refer to various texts developed by UNCITRAL and that such term also appeared in the decision of the Commission adopting the *UNCITRAL Legislative Guide on Insolvency Law for Micro- and Small Enterprises*.[16] Suggestions to replace the term "standard" with "standardization guidelines" or "best practices" did not receive sufficient report.

102. After discussion, the Commission adopted recommendation 9 as follows:

"In order to address MSMEs' financial needs in the context of insolvency, the law should reflect international standards such as those found in the *UNCITRAL Legislative Guide on Insolvency Law* and the *UNCITRAL Legislative Guide on Insolvency Law for Micro- and Small Enterprises*."

Recommendation 10

103. To ensure consistency throughout the draft text (see para. 99 above), the Commission adopted recommendation 10 as follows:

"To help ensure that MSMEs are aware of their rights and obligations, the law should require terms and conditions of the credit agreement to be presented by financers to MSMEs in a clear, understandable and legible way."

Recommendation 11

104. The view was expressed that the draft recommendation seemed incomplete. A proposal was made to widen its scope by adding the phrase "taking into account both the creditor's interest in certainty and predictability with respect to enforcement of its claim for payment and the MSME's interest in understanding the obligation it is incurring and in the avoidance of unfair terms or practices by the creditor." It was,

[15] For example, see General Assembly resolution 77/99, paras. 10 (a) and 20.

[16] A/78/17, para. 135.

however, noted that the related commentary did not discuss creditors' interest but only focused on the interest of the MSME.

105. After discussion, the Commission adopted recommendation 11 as follows:

> "The law should identify both the formalities and content requirements necessary to make a credit agreement effective taking into account the MSME's interest in understanding the obligation it is incurring and in the avoidance of unfair terms or practices."

C. Consideration of the draft commentary

Introduction

Focus and structure of the Guide

106. The Commission agreed to revise the opening sentence of paragraph 12 along the following lines: "The Guide recognizes that, although several features are common to many MSMEs regardless of their size and nature, it is often more challenging for micro- and small enterprises to obtain credit than for medium-sized enterprises. The requirements for micro- and small enterprises to obtain credit (for example, high interest rates, or provision of collateral) may affect smaller MSMEs more severely. High interest rates may make credit unaffordable. In addition, such enterprises may not have collateral of sufficient value to induce creditors to extend credit at lower rates."

Chapter II – Sources of credit and capital available to MSMEs

Friends and family support

107. The Commission agreed to replace the term "owner(s)" with "owner(s) or entrepreneur(s)" in the first and second sentences of paragraph 17.

108. The Commission agreed to add "State laws" after "social norms" in the last sentence of paragraph 18.

Commercial credit

109. The Commission agreed to replace in paragraph 20: the phrase "regulated financial institutions" with "accredited financial institutions".

110. In paragraph 21, for improved clarity and consistency of the text, the Commission agreed to: (a) add the following text before the penultimate sentence: "Most traditional financial service providers do not operate at the micro level. However, where microloan programmes exist, ..."; and (b) replace the term "microlenders" with "microcredit providers" used in paragraph 49 of the draft guide.

Leasing

111. The Commission agreed to revise the first sentence in paragraph 37 as follows:

> "Leasing may become a costly financing option for MSMEs if the legal basis for the lessor's right to repossession on default is inadequate, or if there is no public registration requirement, as it is required for certain leases in the Model Law on Secured Transactions, to reduce the risk of an unauthorized sale of the leased assets by the lessee."

112. The Commission agreed to replace the term "regulated financial institutions" with "accredited financial institutions" in the penultimate sentence of paragraph 37.

Warehouse receipt financing

113. The Commission agreed to insert the following sentence after the first sentence in paragraph 41: "The receipt itself may be valuable collateral because it may give its

holder a right to the goods themselves". It was noted that the word "may" was used in order to accommodate both negotiable and non-negotiable warehouse receipts.

Letters of credit

114. The Commission agreed to replace the last sentence of paragraph 43 with two sentences below:

> "As in the case of the UCP, the international standby practices (ISP 98), also prepared by the ICC, may be incorporated by reference in standby letters of credit. Additionally, in the case of demand guarantees, which fulfil an economic function similar to that of standby letters of credit, the *Uniform Rules for Demand Guarantees*, prepared by the ICC, may be incorporated by reference."

Collective credit and savings arrangements

115. The Commission agreed to replace the second sentence of paragraph 45 with the following sentence: "They are formally regulated organizations jointly owned and controlled by their members, and are often non-profit."

116. The Commission agreed to replace the term "cooperative banks" with "credit cooperatives" in the last sentence of paragraph 45.

Public financial institutions

117. The Commission agreed to delete the phrase "(often, albeit not always owned by the State)" in the first sentence of paragraph 51.

118. The Commission agreed to replace the term "market gaps" with "finance gaps" in the third sentence of paragraph 51.

Chapter III – Measures to facilitate MSMEs' access to credit

Introductory paragraphs

119. The Commission agreed to replace the term "young entrepreneurs" with "start-up entrepreneurs" in paragraph 55.

120. The Commission agreed to replace the second sentence in paragraph 56 with the following sentences: "It will not, however, by itself remove all those obstacles. A combination of regulatory and policy measures can ease the effect of some of these obstacles."

121. The Commission agreed to insert the phrase "and makes recommendations on" before the word "examines" in the first sentence of paragraph 57.

Secured transactions

122. The Commission agreed to replace the phrase "a series of legislative texts" with "a series of texts" in the first sentence of paragraph 73 and to insert the following sentence at the end of that paragraph:

> "The UNIDROIT Model Law on Factoring adopted in 2023 has the same objectives and its provisions are generally consistent with the *UNCITRAL Model Law on Secured Transactions* (2016) and the *United Nations Convention on the Assignment of Receivables in International Trade* (2001)."

123. The Commission agreed to replace in paragraph 75 the phrase "public security rights registry" with "publicly accessible security rights registry".

124. The Commission agreed to replace the phrase "give possession" with "give actual possession" in the third sentence of paragraph 76.

125. The Commission agreed to insert the following sentence at the end of paragraph 81: "It would thus function as a reference point for determining the existence and priority of security rights in such registry."

126. The Commission agreed to place paragraph 91 after paragraph 92 in line with its decision on the corresponding recommendation (see para. 97 above). The Commission also agreed to replace the phrase "prompt realization" with "prompt and economically efficient realization."

127. The Commission agreed to delete the last sentence of paragraph 92.

Personal guarantees

128. The Commission heard a proposal to consolidate paragraphs 98 and 99 into one paragraph so as to eliminate overlapping, and reorganize paragraphs 103 to 105 for improved clarity and consistency of the section. After discussion, the Commission agreed to incorporate the following changes:

(a) To revise paragraph 98 along the following lines:

> "A personal guarantee is a promise by a third party to fulfil the obligations of a debtor to a creditor. Financers may not be prepared to lend money to a MSME without a guarantee of performance by a reliable third party because the risk of loss from the MSME's default would be relatively too high for the financer to bear. The existence of such a guarantee can increase access to credit in two ways. First, if the guarantor is assessed to be able to satisfy the obligation, this can eliminate or lower the creditor's risk of suffering a loss as a result of the debtor's default and, thus, may enable the extension of credit to the debtor where it would not otherwise be available, or lower the cost of that credit, even where the debtor is unable to supply sufficient collateral to bring about those benefits under the applicable secured transactions regime. Although they should not replace a proper credit risk analysis, personal guarantees incentivize financers to extend credit to MSMEs – often at more favourable terms such as a lower interest rate, a larger loan amount or a longer repayment term. This can support and further improve MSME's competitiveness on the market. Second, the prospect of the guarantor being liable for the debt will often provide the guarantor with an incentive to assure that the debtor satisfies its debt so that the guarantor will not have to do so.";

(b) To delete paragraph 99;

(c) To move paragraphs 103 and 104 after the revised paragraph 98, since they addressed issues not only relevant for suretyships, and to delete the subheading "Suretyships for MSMEs";

(d) To delete paragraph 105 since the discussion on surety bonds could be misleading;

(e) To amend the heading of subsection (b) to read "Key features of a personal guarantee regime";

(f) To change the heading above paragraph 107 to "Formal requirements of the personal guarantee".

129. Given the reorganization of the section, it was suggested that the secretariat should have discretion to further review and edit it to improve internal consistency as well as consistency with recommendation 7.

Credit guarantee schemes

130. The Commission agreed to revise the title above paragraph 116 to "Public credit guarantee schemes" since, after the changes that had been agreed upon by the Working Group at its thirty-ninth session (New York, 13–17 February 2023),[17] the section focused only on that type of credit guarantee schemes.

---

[17] See A/CN.9/1128, paras. 33–36.

Assessment of MSMEs' creditworthiness

131. The Commission agreed to revise the title of subsection (b), above paragraph 144, to "Integrating available information", as suggested in footnote 61.

Transparency and other fair lending practices

132. The Commission agreed to delete the last sentence in paragraph 176 given that such a sentence would need to be updated in line with the progress made in UNCITRAL Working Group IV, which would not be feasible after the adoption and publication of the guide. A suggestion to change the title of the section to "Digital environment" did not receive sufficient support, because it was considered that the term "electronic" was broader in scope and would include "digital" aspects.

Other measures to enhance MSME's access to credit: financial literacy

133. The Commission agreed to replace the first sentence in paragraph 189 with the following sentence: "Regulators play a leading role in facilitating access to credit for MSMEs.".

134. A suggestion to insert the word "may" before the phrase "play a leading role" did not receive sufficient support because there was agreement on the need for regulatory and supervisory bodies to play such a leading role, as underscored by the use of the verb "must", rather than "may", in the second sentence of paragraph 189. A suggestion to replace the word "facilitating" with "determining" did not receive sufficient support. It was explained that "determining" implied a more directive power of actually affording access to credit, which would not be appropriate in the context.

D. Adoption of the UNCITRAL Guide on Access to Credit for Micro-, Small and Medium-sized Enterprises

135. After completing its consideration of the draft guide, the Commission adopted by consensus the following decision at its 1192nd meeting, on 11 July 2023:

"*The United Nations Commission on International Trade Law*,

"*Recalling* its mandate under General Assembly resolution 2205 (XXI) of 17 December 1966 to further the progressive harmonization and unification of the law of international trade and in that respect to bear in mind the interests of all peoples, in particular those of developing countries, in the extensive development of international trade,

"*Recalling also* the mandate given to Working Group I (Micro-, Small and Medium-sized Enterprises), in 2013,[18] to work on reducing the legal obstacles faced by micro-, small and medium-sized enterprises throughout their life cycle, in particular in developing economies, and its decision, in 2019,[19] that Working Group I should strengthen and complete that work by addressing the topic of access to credit for micro-, small and medium-sized enterprises,

"*Recalling further* General Assembly resolution 77/160 of 14 December 2022, entitled 'Entrepreneurship for Sustainable Development', which recognizes the importance of encouraging the participation and growth of micro-, small and medium-sized enterprises in international, regional and national markets, including through access to financial services such as affordable microfinance and credit,

"*Aware* of the significant unmet demand for financing from micro-, small and medium-sized enterprises, in particular those owned by women,

[18] A/68/17, paras. 316–322.

[19] A/74/17, para. 192 (a).

"*Mindful* of the many obstacles faced by micro-, small and medium-sized enterprises in obtaining financing because of their small size and other particular features,

"*Recognizing* that a combination of private or commercial law, regulatory and policy measures may help remove many of those obstacles as well as reduce the credit risk faced by financers when lending to micro-, small and medium-sized enterprises,

"*Convinced* that the guidance provided by the UNCITRAL texts on simplification of business incorporation and registration, simplified legal forms for micro-, small and medium-sized enterprises, security interests and insolvency for micro- and small enterprises can assist States in creating a sound legal framework that promotes access to credit for small businesses,

"*Expressing its appreciation* to Working Group I for its work in developing the draft guide on access to credit for micro-, small and medium-sized enterprises and to relevant international intergovernmental and non-governmental organizations for their support and participation,

"1. *Adopts* the recommendations on access to credit for micro-, small and medium-sized enterprises, annexed to the report of the United Nations Commission on International Trade Law on the work of its fifty-sixth session;[20]

"2. *Approves* in principle the draft commentary to the recommendations contained in document A/CN.9/1156, as revised by the Commission at its fifty-sixth session, and authorizes the secretariat to edit and finalize the text of the commentary in light of those revisions;

"3. *Requests* the Secretary-General to publish the recommendations and the commentary as the *UNCITRAL Guide on Access to Credit for Micro-, Small and Medium-sized Enterprises*, as part of the UNCITRAL MSME series, including electronically, in the six official languages of the United Nations, and to disseminate it, together with any relevant information materials, so as to make it widely known and available to Governments and other interested bodies;

"4. *Recommends* that States give due consideration to the *Guide* when adopting or revising legislation relevant to access to credit by micro-, small and medium-sized enterprises, and encourages States to ensure that all such enterprises have equal access to credit."

VI. Consideration of the draft guidance text on early dismissal and preliminary determination

136. The Commission recalled that, at its fifty-fourth session, in 2021, it had requested Working Group II to consider the topic of early dismissal and preliminary determination and present the results of its discussions to the fifty-fifth session of the Commission in 2022.[21] Accordingly, at its seventy-fourth session (Vienna, 27 September–1 October 2021), Working Group II considered the topic based on a note by the Secretariat (A/CN.9/WG.II/WP.220) and requested the Commission to provide guidance on the appropriate form of such work (A/CN.9/1085, paras. 66 and 67).

137. The Commission also recalled that, at its fifty-fifth session, in 2022, it had considered the topic based on a note by the Secretariat containing three legislative options (A/CN.9/1114) and had requested the Working Group to develop a guidance text on early dismissal and preliminary determination on the basis of the first option outlined in A/CN.9/1114.[22] The Working Group considered a draft guidance note on early dismissal and preliminary determination during its seventy-sixth session (Vienna, 10–14 October

[20] A/78/17, annex V.

[21] A/76/17, paras. 25 (g), 186, 214 (b) and 242.

[22] A/77/17, paras. 22 (c), 194 (b) and 229.

2022) and completed its deliberations during the seventy-seventh session (New York, 6–10 February 2023) on the basis of a note by the Secretariat (A/CN.9/WG.II/WP.230).

138. At the present session, the Commission had before it a draft guidance text on early dismissal and preliminary determination as a note for inclusion in the UNCITRAL Notes on Organizing Arbitral Proceedings adopted in 2016 (the "Notes") (A/CN.9/1145).

139. A suggestion to clarify in the draft guidance text the review standards and periods of the two stages of the early dismissal request did not receive support. The draft guidance text was approved as contained in A/CN.9/1145, paras. 6–13, without change.

140. Concerning the new title of the Notes, where the adopted text would appear as note 21, the Commission noted that the Working Group had agreed to propose the title "The UNCITRAL Notes on Organizing Arbitral Proceedings adopted in 2016 (with an additional note on early dismissal and preliminary determination adopted in 2023)".

141. The view was expressed that the proposed title placed too much emphasis on early dismissal and preliminary determination and was not user-friendly. As an alternative, the following shorter title was suggested: "UNCITRAL Notes on Organizing Arbitral Proceedings as amended in 2023". In response, it was said that the proposed new title would suggest that the Notes had been amended in their entirety, whereas only one note had been added. After discussion, the Commission agreed to amend the title of the Notes as suggested by the Working Group.

142. After completing its consideration of the draft guidance text on early dismissal and preliminary determination, the Commission adopted at its 1197th meeting, on 14 July 2023, the following decision:

"*The United Nations Commission on International Trade Law*,

"*Recalling* its mandate under General Assembly resolution 2205 (XXI) of 17 December 1966 to further the progressive harmonization and unification of the law of international trade and in that respect to bear in mind the interests of all peoples, in particular those of developing countries, in the extensive development of international trade,

"*Reaffirming* the value and increased use of arbitration as a method of settling disputes,

"*Recalling* its decision at its forty-ninth session that the purpose of the UNCITRAL Notes on Organizing Arbitral Proceedings[23] is to list and briefly describe matters relevant to the organization of arbitral proceedings,[24]

"*Observing* that the topic of early dismissal and preliminary determination is a significant issue in international commercial arbitration, which should therefore be addressed in the UNCITRAL Notes on Organizing Arbitral Proceedings,

"*Noting* that the preparation of the note on early dismissal and preliminary determination benefited greatly from consultations with Governments and interested intergovernmental and international non-governmental organizations active in the field of arbitration, including arbitral institutions,

"*Expressing its appreciation* to Working Group II for formulating the draft note on early dismissal and preliminary determination,

"1. *Adopts* the guidance text on early dismissal and preliminary determination, as it appears in annex VII of the report of the United Nations

[23] UNCITRAL Notes on Organizing Arbitral Proceedings (2016).

[24] *Official Records of the General Assembly, Seventy-first Session*, Supplement No. 17 (A/71/17), para. 158

Commission on International Trade Law on the work of its fifty-sixth session,[25] for inclusion as note 21 in the newly entitled 'UNCITRAL Notes on Organizing Arbitral Proceedings adopted in 2016 (with an additional note on early dismissal and preliminary determination adopted in 2023)';

"2. *Recommends* the use of the UNCITRAL Notes on Organizing Arbitral Proceedings adopted in 2016 (with an additional note on early dismissal and preliminary determination adopted in 2023) by parties to arbitration, arbitral tribunals, arbitral institutions as well as for academic and training purposes with respect to international commercial dispute settlement;

"3. *Requests* the Secretary-General to publish the UNCITRAL Notes on Organizing Arbitral Proceedings adopted in 2016 (with an additional note on early dismissal and preliminary determination adopted in 2023), including electronically, and in the six official languages of the United Nations, and to make all efforts to ensure that the Notes become generally known and available."

VII. Dispute settlement: progress report of Working Group II

143. The Commission recalled that, at its fifty-fifth session, in 2022, it had entrusted the Working Group with the consideration of the topics of technology-related dispute resolution and adjudication jointly and also with the consideration of ways to further accelerate the resolution of disputes. It had been agreed that the work should build on the UNCITRAL Expedited Arbitration Rules and that the model provisions or clauses, or other forms of legislative or non-legislative text could be prepared on matters such as shorter time frames, the appointment of experts/neutrals, confidentiality, and the legal nature of the outcome of the proceedings, all of which would allow disputing parties to tailor the proceeding to their needs to further expedite the proceedings.[26]

144. The Commission was informed that Working Group II, at its seventy-sixth session, had commenced deliberations on the topics of technology-related dispute resolution and adjudication on the basis of a note by the Secretariat (A/CN.9/WG.II/WP.227) that contained draft model clauses. The Commission was further informed that Working Group II had continued considering those topics at its seventy-seventh session based on a note by the Secretariat (A/CN.9/WG.II/WP.231). The Commission was also informed of the consultations with experts and users that had taken place between the Working Group sessions. The Commission had before it the reports of Working Group II (Dispute Settlement) on the work of its seventy-sixth (Vienna, 10–14 October 2022) (A/CN.9/1123) and seventy-seventh sessions (New York, 6–10 February 2023) (A/CN.9/1129). Those reports also covered the discussions on early dismissal and preliminary determination, which resulted in the adoption by the Commission at the present session of the guidance text on that subject (see para. 142 above and annex VII to the present report).

145. The Commission expressed its satisfaction with the progress made by Working Group II and the support provided by the secretariat.

VIII. Investor-State dispute settlement reform: progress report of Working Group III

146. The Commission recalled that, at its fiftieth session, in 2017, it had entrusted Working Group III with a broad mandate to work on the possible reform of investor-State dispute settlement.[27] The Commission took note of the progress being made by Working Group III in the third phase of its mandate, which was to develop concrete reform elements to be recommended to the Commission, with the first set of

[25] A/78/17.

[26] A/77/17, paras. 223–225.

[27] A/72/17, para. 264.

reform elements finalized and adopted by the Commission at the present session (see chap. IV).

147. Taking into account the reports of Working Group III on the work of its forty-third, forty-fourth and forty-fifth sessions (A/CN.9/1124, A/CN.9/1130 and A/CN.9/1131, respectively), the Commission commended the Working Group for completing its work on the draft codes of conduct for arbitrators and judges in international investment dispute resolution and the respective commentaries, the draft provisions on mediation and the draft guidelines on investment mediation. The Commission also noted that progress was being made with regard to other reform elements, including the establishment of an advisory centre on international investment law, an appellate mechanism, a multilateral instrument on investor-State dispute settlement reform, dispute prevention and mitigation, a number of procedural and cross-cutting issues and the selection and appointment of tribunal members of a standing multilateral mechanism. The Commission further noted that progress was being made through a series of intersessional meetings and other informal meetings.[28] In that context, it was mentioned that an intersessional meeting of Working Group III would be held in Singapore, on 7 and 8 September 2023, on topics relating to the possible establishment of a standing mechanism and an appellate mechanism. During those deliberations, the Government of Thailand expressed an interest in hosting an intersessional meeting in the near future.

148. The Commission expressed its appreciation to the secretariat for closely cooperating with the secretariat of the International Centre for Settlement of Investment Disputes on the draft codes of conduct and with the World Bank Group regarding dispute prevention and mitigation. The Commission also commended the secretariat for its participation at events organized by the Organisation for Economic Co-operation and Development (OECD), as well as for coordinating generally with international governmental and non-governmental organizations to hold a number of side events on a range of topics during the sessions of the Working Group.

149. The Commission recalled that the General Assembly, on 24 December 2021, had decided to allocate an additional one-week session per year to the Commission and the necessary human resources to the secretariat to support the work of Working Group III.[29] The Commission further recalled that, when it had made the recommendation to the General Assembly for the additional resources, it decided to re-evaluate and, if needed, revisit its decision concerning the need for allocating an additional one-week session per year and supporting resources to the Working Group, taking into consideration the Working Group's report on the use of its resources.[30]

150. Accordingly, the Commission was informed that the additional conference time of one week allocated respectively for 2022 and 2023 had been utilized by the Working Group to hold a two-week forty-third session in September 2022 and a one-week forty-fourth session in January 2023, both in Vienna.[31] The Commission was further informed that the secretariat had filled the three additional posts allocated in 2022. It was observed that the additional conference time and the human resources allowed the Working Group to complete its consideration of the draft codes of conduct and the draft texts on mediation, which were submitted to the Commission this year.

151. The Chair of Working Group III provided an outline of the work to be conducted by the Working Group during the three weeks of sessions scheduled until the fifty-seventh session of the Commission and indicated that the Working Group would aim to submit the draft provisions on an advisory centre on international investment

[28] Information about informal meetings is available on the web page of Working Group III (https://uncitral.un.org/en/working_groups/3/investor-state) in the right-hand column under "Inter-sessional Activities".

[29] General Assembly resolution 76/229, para. 15.

[30] A/76/17, para. 263.

[31] A/77/17, para. 321.

law and a guidance text on means to prevent and mitigate disputes for consideration by the Commission at its next session.

152. The Commission reiterated that progress should continue to be made in accordance with the revised workplan prepared by the Working Group at its resumed fortieth session, in May 2021 (A/CN.9/1054, annex). While emphasizing the need to take a flexible approach in carrying out the work and to adapt the workplan to the current needs of the Working Group, the Commission requested the Working Group to continue its work in an effective manner and encouraged it to present the outcome of the above-mentioned work at its next session in 2024.

153. The Commission took further note of the outreach activities of the secretariat aimed at raising awareness about the work of the Working Group and ensuring that the process would remain inclusive and fully transparent. The Commission also commended the secretariat for updating the Working Group III web page to provide relevant information to the delegates in a concise and timely manner.

154. The Commission expressed its appreciation for the financial support provided by the Governments of France and Germany, the European Union and the Swiss Agency for Development and Cooperation. The Commission called for continued support by the donors for travel and simultaneous interpretation to ensure inclusiveness of the Working Group deliberations, and for post-related costs to enhance the capacities of the secretariat.

155. After discussion, the Commission expressed its satisfaction with the progress made by Working Group III and the support provided by the secretariat to the Working Group.

IX. Electronic commerce: progress report of Working Group IV

156. The Commission recalled that, at its fifty-fifth session, in 2022, it had mandated Working Group IV to proceed with work on data provision contracts in tandem with work on the use of artificial intelligence and automation in contracting.[32] At the present session, the Commission had before it the reports of the Working Group on the work of its sixty-fourth session (Vienna, 31 October–4 November 2022) and sixty-fifth session (New York, 10–14 April 2023) (A/CN.9/1125 and A/CN.9/1132, respectively).

157. The Commission expressed its satisfaction with the progress made by the Working Group in its consideration of those topics. It also expressed its appreciation to the European Law Institute for partnering with the secretariat in holding the intersessional event on automated contracting on 17 January 2023, which helped the Working Group to move beyond theoretical issues and focus on technical issues related to the topic.

158. The Commission noted that, at its most recent session, the Working Group advanced the development of normative texts on both topics, namely a set of default rules on data provision contracts and principles on automated contracting. It invited the Working Group to continue working on both topics in parallel at its forthcoming sessions, on the basis of a revised set of texts to be prepared by the secretariat. It heard that the secretariat would continue compiling information on the use of data provision contracts and automated contracting in practice and continue to monitor other international initiatives that intersect with both topics.

159. The Commission was reminded of the views that had been expressed at its fifty-fifth session on the need to avoid intellectual property issues, and to avoid overlap with work being carried out within the United Nations system and other international forums, such as work aimed at developing harmonized standards on the ethical use and governance of artificial intelligence and work on personal data protection. It was also informed about the approach proposed within the Working

[32] A/77/17, para. 163.

Group (A/CN.9/1132, para. 24) by which intersections with those issues could be addressed by expressly preserving and prioritizing the application of laws dealing specifically with those issues.

X. Insolvency law: progress report of Working Group V

160. The Commission had before it the reports of Working Group V on the work of its sixty-first session (Vienna, 12–16 December 2022) and sixty-second session (New York, 17–20 April 2023) (A/CN.9/1126 and A/CN.9/1133, respectively). It noted with appreciation that a half-day conference commemorating the twenty-fifth anniversary of the UNCITRAL Model Law on Cross-Border Insolvency (1997)[33] had been held on the last day of the sixty-first session of the Working Group before the adoption of the report of the session,[34] complementing the panel discussion on "Sharing experience across regions: insolvency reforms in Latin America, Europe and beyond", held on 15 July 2022 during the fifty-fifth session of the Commission.[35] The Commission also noted with appreciation that a half-day conference dedicated to the fifth anniversary of the UNCITRAL Model Law on Recognition and Enforcement of Insolvency-Related Judgments (2018)[36] had been held on 21 April 2023,[37] the originally scheduled last day of the sixty-second session of the Working Group that had to be shortened due to the changes introduced in the date of observance of a United Nations official holiday in New York in April 2023.[38]

161. While regretting the shortening of the Working Group session, the Commission expressed its appreciation to the International Insolvency Institute and the United States Bankruptcy Court for the Southern District of New York for having organized and hosted that important and informative commemorative event. It also commended the secretariat for supporting the event and making other adjustments that ensured the productive use of all five dates originally allocated to the session. In particular, the Commission noted with appreciation that, in line with the decisions of the Commission at its fifty-fifth session,[39] adjustments had been made to allow the Working Group to adopt the report of the sixty-second session through a written procedure, thereby enabling deliberations during the full four days left available for the session.

162. The Commission took note of the progress achieved by the Working Group in the consideration of the topics of civil asset tracing and recovery and applicable law in insolvency proceedings. It expressed its support and appreciation to the Working Group and the secretariat for continuing treating both topics equally, in conformity with the mandate given to the Working Group,[40] and commended the high quality of the papers prepared by the secretariat.[41]

163. As regards the topic of civil asset tracing and recovery, the Commission commended the Working Group for completing the review of: (a) an inventory of civil asset tracing and recovery tools in insolvency proceedings that reflected submissions by States; and (b) the first draft of an educational and informational text that reflected the results of the secretariat's exploratory and preparatory work and inputs received from States and experts on the topic. The Commission took note of proposals made in the Working Group, including as regards preparation of a toolkit that would aim at expediting asset tracing and recovery in cross-border insolvencies.[42] The view was

---

[33] General Assembly resolution 52/158, annex.

[34] The summary of the conference is contained in A/CN.9/1126, annex.

[35] A/77/17, para. 263. The summary of the panel discussion is contained in A/CN.9/WG.V/WP.184.

[36] United Nations publication, Sales No. E.19.V.8.

[37] The materials of the Conference may be found at https://uncitral.un.org/en/5MLIJ.

[38] A/CN.9/1126, paras. 83–86.

[39] A/77/17, para. 236.

[40] A/76/17, para. 217.

[41] A/CN.9/WG.V/WP.182, A/CN.9/WG.V/WP.182/Add.1, A/CN.9/WG.V/WP.183, A/CN.9/WG.V/WP.183/Add.1, A/CN.9/WG.V/WP.186 and A/CN.9/WG.V/WP.187.

[42] A/CN.9/1133, annex.

expressed that the work product on asset tracing and recovery in insolvency proceedings should stay educational and informational but could, at the same time, be flexible and include a toolkit for reference by States. The Commission noted that the Working Group, at its next sessions, was expected to consider issues arising from tracing and recovering digital assets in insolvency proceedings as well as issues related to the proposed toolkit.

164. As regards the topic of applicable law in insolvency proceedings, the Commission noted that the Working Group continued considering draft legislative provisions and commentary in the context of a single domestic insolvency proceeding, and that so far the deliberations had not encompassed issues arising from applicable law in concurrent proceedings with respect to the same debtor or in the enterprise group context. The Commission noted with satisfaction that some progress had been achieved towards resolving outstanding matters related to possible additional exceptions to the envisaged default rule for the law governing effects of insolvency proceedings (in addition to the already envisaged exceptions for labour contracts and for payment and settlement systems and regulated financial markets). The Commission noted the intention of the Working Group to continue discussing those matters, possibly in conjunction with issues arising from applicable law in cross-border insolvency recognition and enforcement, as well as outstanding matters related to the envisaged exception for payment and settlement systems and regulated financial markets. The view was expressed that the work on the topic would produce a significant impact on domestic laws and practices as regards applicable law in insolvency proceedings and that it should be completed expeditiously. The Commission acknowledged that the applicable law project touched upon many areas of law, including broad and complex issues. It noted that some unresolved issues were fundamental, such as those related to secured transactions, and required thorough consideration by the Working Group.

165. The Commission took note of the recently completed and continuing work in other forums on topics of relevance to its texts on insolvency law and the current work of the Working Group. It expressed its appreciation to the secretariat for bringing pertinent issues to the attention of the Working Group and otherwise ensuring a close coordination and cooperation with relevant institutions, in line with the Commission's decision.[43] To enable such continued coordination and cooperation, organize expert consultations and ensure timely preparation and issuance of the Working Group's working papers, the Commission considered that more time should be allocated between session of the Working Group.

166. The Commission welcomed the publication in the six languages of the United Nations of its text on insolvency law for micro- and small enterprises adopted in 2021. It expressed appreciation to the secretariat for having prepared that publication, as the Commission had envisaged, in the form of a stand-alone text (part of the UNCITRAL MSMEs text series)[44] and as part five of the *UNCITRAL Legislative Guide on Insolvency Law*.[45] The Commission commended the secretariat for preparing, in conjunction with that publication, online tables of concordance between recommendations related to standard insolvency regime and recommendations related to a simplified insolvency regime, also in the six languages of the United Nations.[46]

[43] A/77/17, para. 190.

[44] United Nations publication, 2022.

[45] United Nations publication, 2022.

[46] The online table of concordance accompanying the stand-alone text may be found at https://uncitral.un.org/en/insolvency_table_of_concordance_mses. The online table of concordance accompanying part five of the *UNCITRAL Legislative Guide on Insolvency Law* may be found at https://uncitral.un.org/en/insolvency_table_of_concordance_part_5.

XI. Negotiable multimodal transport documents: progress report of Working Group VI

167. The Commission recalled that, at its fifty-fifth session, in 2022, it had decided to assign the topic of negotiable multimodal transport documents to Working Group VI.[47] The Commission had before it the reports of Working Group VI on the work of its forty-first session (Vienna, 28 November–2 December 2022) (A/CN.9/1127) and forty-second session (New York, 8–12 May 2023) (A/CN.9/1134).

168. The Commission was informed that Working Group VI had commenced its deliberations on the basis of a set of preliminary draft provisions for an instrument on negotiable cargo documents prepared by the secretariat. The instrument was intended to enable the issuance of documents of title representing goods received for international carriage irrespective of the actual modes of transportation used for the particular carriage, which would be used for financing purposes. Working Group VI had begun with a general exchange of views on the objectives, scope and form of the proposed new instrument, and proceeded with an article-by-article review of the preliminary draft provisions. The Commission took note of the decision of the Working Group to postpone its consideration of draft provisions on electronic aspects and revisit them after finalizing the substantive provisions concerning negotiability.

169. The Commission noted that broad support had been expressed for negotiable cargo documents to be issued by any transport operator acting as a contractual carrier, irrespective of whether or not that person performed the carriage itself. The Commission also noted that there had been support for the proposition that, as a default rule, the transport document should serve as a negotiable cargo document by inserting on its face an appropriate reference to the draft new instrument, and that as a fallback rule, in the event that no transport document had been issued or that domestic laws prohibited the transport document to function as a negotiable document, the negotiable cargo document could be issued as a separate document in addition to the transport document. In that connection, it had been observed that a negotiable cargo document issued as a separate document would not substitute any transport document which the transport operator might be required to issue. There was support within the Commission for the Working Group to pursue the so-called "dual track" approach and to focus on the negotiability function of cargo documents.

170. The Commission noted that the new instrument currently being considered by the Working Group contained draft provisions dealing with the issuance, legal effect and transferability of electronic negotiable cargo records. The Commission reiterated the need to ensure a consistency of approach not only with existing instruments, such as the UNCITRAL Model Law on Electronic Transferable Records,[48] but also among various projects that included electronic commerce aspects, such as the joint UNCITRAL/UNIDROIT model law on warehouse receipts (see paras. 175–177 below). The Commission stressed that it was important to avoid unnecessary duplication of provisions dealing with essentially the same legal questions, and, more crucially, to prevent fragmentation of provisions and concepts dealing with electronic transferable records. At the same time, the Commission also noted that a new instrument on negotiable cargo documents could take the form of an international convention and heard the view that in such case it might not be feasible to assume that a model law – even if widely implemented – could on all instances be relied upon to supplement the legal regime established by an international convention. The Commission recognized that the paramount consideration should in any event be the need to ensure consistency between the future instrument and existing UNCITRAL texts, in particular the UNCITRAL Model Law on Electronic Transferable Records. It was also noted that the Working Group must continue to be mindful of creating

[47] A/77/17, para. 202.

[48] United Nations publication, Sales No. E.17.V.5.

legal risks for private parties, including such parties not directly involved in creating or transferring negotiable cargo documents.

171. The Commission expressed its satisfaction with the progress made by Working Group VI and the support provided by the secretariat (see also para. 174 (f) below).

XII. Work programme

172. The Commission recalled its agreement to reserve time for discussion of its overall work programme as a separate topic at each session, to facilitate the effective planning of its activities.[49]

173. The Commission took note of the documents prepared to assist its discussions on the topic (A/CN.9/1140 and the documents referred to therein, including the proposals contained in documents A/CN.9/1144, A/CN.9/1146, A/CN.9/1152, A/CN.9/1153, A/CN.9/1153/Add.1, A/CN.9/1154 and A/CN.9/1155) and of lists of activities of the secretariat planned until the fifty-seventh session of the Commission in support of the legislative work by the Commission and its working groups.

A. Legislative programme under consideration by working groups

174. The Commission took note of the progress of its working groups as reported earlier in the session (see chapters VII to XI of the present report), reaffirmed the programme of current legislative activities set out in table 1 of document A/CN.9/1140, with the assignment of one new topic, as follows:

(a) The Commission agreed to entrust Working Group I with the preparation of a draft model law on warehouse receipts and to use the draft set out in the annex to the relevant note by the Secretariat (A/CN.9/1152) as a basis for its deliberations;

(b) With respect to dispute settlement, the Commission agreed that Working Group II should continue its consideration of the topics of technology-related dispute resolution and adjudication;

(c) With respect to investor-State dispute settlement reform, the Commission agreed that Working Group III should continue with its work programme as mandated;

(d) With respect to electronic commerce, the Commission confirmed that Working Group IV should continue working in parallel on the formulation of default rules on data provision contracts and principles on automated contracting;

(e) With respect to insolvency law, the Commission agreed that Working Group V should continue its consideration of legal issues arising from civil asset tracing and recovery in insolvency proceedings as well as of the topic of applicable law in insolvency proceedings; and

(f) With respect to negotiable cargo documents (previously referred to as "negotiable multimodal transport documents"), the Commission agreed that Working Group VI should continue its consideration of a new international instrument on negotiable cargo documents.

B. Additional topics considered at earlier sessions of the Commission

1. Warehouse receipts

175. The Commission recalled that it had decided to place the topic of warehouse receipt financing on its work programme at its forty-ninth session, in 2016.[50] The Commission also recalled that it had considered progress reports by the secretariat at

---

[49] A/68/17, para. 310.

[50] A/71/17, para. 125.

its fifty-first session, in 2018,[51] at its fifty-second session, in 2019,[52] and at its fifty-third session, in 2020, when the Commission endorsed the recommendations set out in the relevant note by the Secretariat concerning the scope of the project, the possible content of a model law on the private law aspects of warehouse receipts as well as the methodology for such work, in particular that it be carried out jointly with UNIDROIT.[53] The Commission also recalled that, at its fifty-fourth session, in 2021, it had been informed, that the Working Group on a Model Law on Warehouse Receipts convened by UNIDROIT in consultation with the UNCITRAL secretariat estimated that more than two sessions would still be needed before it could submit a preliminary draft model law on warehouse receipts for consideration by the UNIDROIT Governing Council, possibly at its 102nd session, in 2023, and subsequent transmittal to the first available UNCITRAL working group.[54]

176. The Commission also recalled that, at its fifty-fifth session, in 2022, it had considered a note by the Secretariat outlining the progress made by the joint UNIDROIT/UNCITRAL Working Group on a Model Law on Warehouse Receipts since the fifty-fourth session of the Commission (A/CN.9/1102). At that session, the Commission had noted the technical difficulty of formulating rules acceptable to different legal systems and the complex issues raised by negotiable instruments and stressed the importance for the working group of adopting technological neutrality and functional equivalence as basic principles for its drafting effort.[55]

177. At the present session, the Commission had before it a note by the Secretariat on the progress made by the Working Group since the fifty-fifth session of the Commission (A/CN.9/1152). The Commission was informed that a draft model law on warehouse receipts had been finalized by the joint UNIDROIT/UNCITRAL Working Group and that the UNIDROIT Governing Council, at its 102nd session (Rome, 10–12 May 2023), had agreed that the draft was ready for submission to UNCITRAL for State negotiations and completion. The Commission commended its secretariat and UNIDROIT for the work already accomplished, noting that it was the result of a good and effective coordination and cooperation between UNCITRAL and UNIDROIT, which should continue throughout the preparation of a draft guide to enactment of the model law on warehouse receipts. While the Commission agreed that the current draft model law accommodated different legal traditions and dealt with the most essential issues for establishing an efficient and predictable regime for warehouse receipts operation and financing, it was observed that the draft model law did not contain rules on important issues such as loss sharing and warehouse operators' liability, which the UNCITRAL working group may wish to include in its discussions. After deliberation, the Commission agreed to refer the draft model law on warehouse receipts to Working Group I. In doing so, the Commission noted the advanced stage of the draft model law on warehouse receipts and expressed its belief that consideration of the text by the Working Group would require only a short amount of time, possibly two sessions.

2. The impact of the coronavirus disease (COVID-19) on international trade law

178. The Commission recalled that it had first considered the topic of the impact of the coronavirus disease (COVID-19) on international trade law at its fifty-third session, in 2020, when it heard a proposal regarding possible future work in connection with measures implemented by States in response to the COVID-19 pandemic. In particular, it had been suggested that the Commission might wish to investigate whether those measures had exposed gaps or obstacles to cross-border trade and investment that could be overcome through work by UNCITRAL in harmonizing cross-border rules

[51] *Official Records of the General Assembly, Seventy-third Session, Supplement No. 17* (A/73/17), para. 249.

[52] A/74/17, paras. 196 and 221 (b).

[53] *Official Records of the General Assembly, Seventy-fifth Session, Supplement No. 17* (A/75/17), part two, paras. 60 and 61.

[54] A/76/17, para. 220.

[55] A/77/17, para. 197.

(see A/CN.9/1039/Rev.1). After discussion, the Commission had requested the secretariat to explore that proposal further.[56]

179. The Commission also recalled that, at its fifty-fourth session, in 2021, it had considered again the topic (on the basis of documents A/CN.9/1080 and A/CN.9/1081) and had requested the secretariat to continue its exploratory work on (a) the issues identified in the progress report as possibly falling within the mandate of UNCITRAL and to continue to hold expert meetings and other events with interested stakeholders to further advance the exploratory work, and (b) the options for establishing an online platform for information exchange by States.[57]

180. The Commission also recalled that, at its fifty-fifth session, in 2022, it had considered a note by the Secretariat setting out further elements relating to the exploratory work regarding, first, issues related to the disruption of the global economy and international trade due to the COVID-19 pandemic, and second, the development of an online platform (A/CN.9/1119). Support had been expressed for the secretariat to continue examining which UNCITRAL texts could be useful to assist MSMEs in a crisis and how UNCITRAL instruments could be utilized to facilitate digital commerce and paperless trade, and thereby reduce trade disruptions and bottlenecks in the event of a future global crisis.[58] The Commission had requested the secretariat to continue its exploratory work on the impact of COVID-19 on international trade by holding expert group meetings and other events with interested stakeholders to further advance such work.[59] As regards the development of an online platform, the Commission had noted that the secretariat had set up a web page containing all of the relevant information related to the project and that the establishment of an interactive platform would require additional resources.[60]

181. At the present session, the Commission had before it a note by the Secretariat on the subject containing in an annex a document tentatively titled “COVID-19 and international trade law instruments: a legal toolkit prepared by the UNCITRAL secretariat” (A/CN.9/1144).

182. The Commission took note of activities undertaken by the secretariat to further advance the exploratory work, in particular: (a) the 2022 UNCITRAL Latin American and Caribbean Days, which explored in 17 States how UNCITRAL instruments could be utilized in preparing MSMEs for a crisis such as the pandemic; (b) the presentation by the secretariat of the preliminary findings of its exploratory work at the Asia-Pacific Economic Cooperation Economic Policy Dialogue, co-chaired by Viet Nam in February 2023; and (c) a hybrid event on the “Impact of the international health crisis on legal infrastructure for trade”, held in Yerevan in June 2023, organized by the Ministry of Foreign Affairs of Armenia and the secretariat, at which experiences and best practices were exchanged and the toolkit was discussed, with the aim of supporting States and other stakeholders in the event of a future health crisis that could similarly impact supply chains and trade flows.

183. It was pointed out that the thematic structure of the toolkit would make access and reference easy for those less acquainted with UNCITRAL instruments by explaining existing UNCITRAL instruments in different areas, such as electronic commerce, insolvency, and dispute resolution and provide for more visibility of UNCITRAL texts. It was observed that the toolkit was a rich source of information, and would be a valuable reference for States and other stakeholders that might have to deal with extraordinary situations in the future. It was suggested that the toolkit be updated, when needed, for instance when the Commission adopted new instruments of relevance for the toolkit.

184. Some suggestions to the toolkit were made, such as (a) adding the possibility of an open framework agreement as per articles 60 and 61 of the UNCITRAL Model Law on

[56] A/75/17, part two, para. 89.
[57] A/76/17, para. 241.
[58] A/77/17, para. 207.
[59] Ibid., paras. 22 (i) and 208.
[60] Ibid., para. 206.

Public Procurement,[61] (b) clarifying in paragraph 52 the origin of the Principles for Effective Insolvency and Creditor/Debtor Regimes, (c) making, in paragraphs 53 and 54, a reference to recommendation 363 of the *UNCITRAL Legislative Guide on Insolvency Law, Part Five – Insolvency Law for Micro- and Small Enterprises* (see para. 166 above) and (d) adding a reference to and explanation of the newly adopted UNCITRAL Guide on Access to Credit for Micro-, Small and Medium-sized Enterprises (see chapter V of this report).

185. After discussion, the Commission commended the contributing States and the secretariat for the work and authorized the secretariat to finalize the text found in the annex of A/CN.9/1144 and publish the finalized text, including electronically, in the six official languages of the United Nations. The Commission encouraged States and other stakeholders to consult the toolkit and the secretariat to use it in its awareness-raising and promotional activities.

3. Climate change mitigation, adaptation and resilience

186. The Commission recalled that, at its fifty-fourth session, in 2021, it had heard a proposal to examine (a) how existing UNCITRAL texts could be aligned with climate change mitigation, adaptation and resilience goals, and (b) whether further work could be done by UNCITRAL to facilitate those goals in the implementation of those texts or through the development of new texts. It had been added that public-private partnerships could be an area of focus for taking stock of existing texts, while legal uncertainty regarding the legal status of carbon credits traded in voluntary carbon markets could be a focus for future legislative work.[62]

187. Broad support had been expressed at that time for the Commission to consider the proposal further, based on more precise information on the work involved. It had been added that member States might need to carry out further internal consultations across different government agencies before a decision on future work could be taken, and that such work would need to be undertaken within existing public international law frameworks, such as the Paris Agreement on climate change of 2015. After discussion, the Commission had requested the secretariat to consult with interested States with a view to developing a more detailed proposal on the topic for presentation to the Commission for its consideration at its next session, in 2022.[63]

188. The Commission recalled that, at its fifty-fifth session, in 2022, it had considered a note by the Secretariat summarizing the findings and recommendations of a study on private law aspects of climate change commissioned from an outside expert with a view to assisting the Commission to consider the desirability and feasibility of undertaking work in that area (A/CN.9/1120 and A/CN.9/1120/Add.1). At that time, there had been wide agreement within the Commission on the importance of the topic and on the usefulness of exploring how UNCITRAL could offer its own contribution to the international community's efforts to combat climate change and mitigate its effects by updating existing private law instruments and developing new enabling legal mechanisms, if necessary.[64] The Commission had requested the secretariat to conduct further research in the area, in consultation with outside experts and interested organizations from both within and outside the United Nations system.[65] It had also requested the secretariat to organize a colloquium or an expert group meeting on the various legal issues surrounding climate change mitigation, adaptation and resilience, in conjunction with relevant and interested international organizations.[66]

189. At the present session, the Commission had before it a note by the Secretariat on the subject (A/CN.9/1153 and A/CN.9/1153/Add.1), which provided additional

---

[61] United Nations publication, Sales No. E.14.V.1.
[62] A/76/17, para. 244.
[63] Ibid., para. 246.
[64] A/77/17, para. 212.
[65] Ibid., para. 216.
[66] Ibid.

information and comments received by the secretariat on the issues discussed in the two notes that the Commission had considered at its fifty-fifth session. The Commission also heard an oral report by the secretariat on the results of the UNCITRAL Colloquium on Climate Change and International Trade Law.

(a) Colloquium on Climate Change and International Trade Law

190. The Commission commended the secretariat for having organized the UNCITRAL Colloquium on Climate Change and International Trade Law, which took place on 12 and 13 July 2023 to consider areas in which international trade law could effectively support the achievement of climate action goals set by the international community, the scope and value of legal harmonization in those areas and the need for international guidance for legislators, policymakers, courts and dispute resolution bodies.

191. The Commission noted that the Colloquium consisted of seven panels involving over 30 speakers and moderators from international intergovernmental and non-governmental organizations, industry and business representatives, academia and private practice from all continents (see annex VI). After a high-level opening session on the role of market and non-market mechanisms under the international framework on climate change, in particular article 6 of the Paris Agreement, the first day of the Colloquium addressed, in particular, regulatory aspects and legal underpinnings of financial instruments to support emission reduction and carbon trading, and the legal nature of voluntary carbon credits and other green investment instruments, their use as collateral and the rights of holders. The second day of the Colloquium considered international, regional and States' efforts to call upon private sector support towards achieving climate goals by advocating and advancing climate-responsible corporate conduct, the various adaptation strategies and approaches available to private sector operators to promote sustainability in their supply chains, and the current trends in climate change disputes and their legal implication for corporate entities to fulfil the duty of care and foster the incorporation of climate considerations into business and investment decisions. The second day of the Colloquium concluded with a round table that included Permanent Representatives of Member States to the Vienna-based international organizations from all regional groups represented at the Commission. During the Colloquium, doubts were expressed as to the feasibility and desirability of proposals made by Colloquium participants.

192. The Commission noted that Colloquium participants had noted the importance of the various topics discussed at the Colloquium and the desirability for UNCITRAL, as an organ of the United Nations General Assembly, to offer its own contribution in the formulation of guidance on those legal questions related to its mandate, which might impact climate action, and to take a leading role in coordinating the contribution that other organizations active in the fields of international trade law, private law and private international law might provide. In view of the wider variety of issues, as illustrated by the broad thematic areas covered by the Colloquium, and a number of complementary or adjacent areas that emerged during the discussion, it was noted among Colloquium participants that, as a first step and in close cooperation with intergovernmental and non-governmental organizations with relevant expertise, in particular UNFCCC, UNIDROIT and HCCH, with the participation of experts representing member States, and paying special attention to the inclusion of developing countries, UNCITRAL could develop a taxonomy for identifying the questions of international trade law, private law and private international law that impact on the implementation and operation of market and non-market emission reduction mechanisms under the international framework on climate change, including both compliance and voluntary carbon markets, as well as issues related to corporate due diligence and disclosure obligations, legal mechanisms for enforcing climate sustainability obligations in international value chains and climate-related dispute settlement mechanisms.

(b) Future work deliberations at the Commission

193. Having taken note of the main topics discussed and the proposals for future work made at the Colloquium as well as the information provided in the background notes submitted by the secretariat to its fifty-fifth session (A/CN.9/1120 and A/CN.9/1120/Add.1) and to the present session (A/CN.9/1153 and A/CN.9/1153/Add.1), the Commission proceeded to consider the desirability and feasibility of work in the area of climate change mitigation, adaptation and resilience and the scope and methodology of such possible work. There was wide agreement as to the timeliness of the topic, the need for the international community to tackle it from various angles and the usefulness of a mapping exercise of relevant questions of international trade law, private law and private international law. It was observed that global efforts to combat climate change were an integral part of the agenda of the United Nations. As stated, therefore, as a subsidiary body of the General Assembly, UNCITRAL should consider undertaking work on those aspects of climate change falling within its mandate, and could support the efforts of other United Nations bodies and Secretariat units in that respect. The views varied, however, as to which topics were appropriate for future work by UNCITRAL and how such work should proceed.

194. The Commission heard a proposal that its work could initially focus on questions of international trade law, private law and private international law that impact on the implementation and operation of voluntary carbon markets. Noting, in particular, that the UNIDROIT General Assembly, 81st session (Rome, 15 December 2022) had agreed to include in the UNIDROIT work programme a project to "analyse the private law aspects and determine the legal nature" of voluntary carbon credits, the Commission was invited to request its secretariat to work in cooperation with UNFCCC, UNIDROIT and HCCH to develop a taxonomy of relevant legal issues involving also other organizations with relevant expertise – many of which had participated in the Colloquium – and to pay special attention to the inclusion of developing countries. To enhance the inclusiveness of such work, the proposal suggested that the UNCITRAL secretariat should request all States Members of the United Nations to nominate experts on legal questions related to climate change, including market and non-market mechanisms for the implementation of article 6 of the Paris Agreement and to present the result of their joint work to the Commission and the UNIDROIT Governing Council, at which stage each organization could decide whether there was scope for any additional work and in which form. The proposal also noted that the contribution of HCCH, which did not yet have a mandate in that area, should also be sought on applicable law issues, subject to its own working methods and governance process.

195. There was wide support within the Commission for the need to ensure consistency and inclusiveness and to avoid overlap and duplication of international efforts in this area. At the same time, however, it was stressed that any work by UNCITRAL should aim at becoming ultimately as acceptable as possible to all Member States, given that not all States Member of the United Nations were also members of UNIDROIT and HCCH. While any collaborative work should respect the respective working methods of the organizations involved, the entire membership of all organizations must have a chance of being involved. In view of the implications of any work on voluntary carbon credits for broader policy issues related to the implementation of international law, including treaties on climate change, there was support for the view that several States, in particular developing countries, needed more time to reflect on the implications of the proposed project and that the Commission should request the secretariat to make detailed concrete proposals for such future work, including its methodology and the mechanisms for obtaining the input of Member States, as well as a systematic review and periodical updates to States (if possible) of relevant initiatives at other forums for consideration by the Commission at a later stage.

196. It was stressed that all regions of the world were likely to be seriously affected by climate change and that developing countries in particular would suffer from its impact and the resulting challenges to their economic and development trajectory.

UNCITRAL, it was said, could also play a role in the fight against climate change and that there would be benefits to greater legal certainty in the area of international trade law. There was strong support for the view that any work to be carried out should be consistent with existing international law, including treaties on climate change, where relevant, in particular the Paris Agreement on climate change of 2015 and UNFCCC.[67] Among the views expressed, it was emphasized that such work should have due regard for the principle of the common but differentiated responsibilities and respective capabilities of States. Finally, it was said that no measures, including unilateral ones, should constitute a means of arbitrary or unjustifiable discrimination in access to climate friendly-technology or a disguised restriction on international trade. The view was expressed that international trade law aspects of economic and financial sanctions or restrictive measures should be discussed under the current agenda for the goods and services related to climate change.

197. A countervailing view was that the concept of common but differentiated responsibilities and respective capabilities of States was not relevant for the work of UNCITRAL on international trade law and that it should not be incorporated into the scope for framing a UNCITRAL project. It was further said that UNCITRAL should not be treated as another forum for engaging in political manoeuvring, and that the serious challenges of climate change should not be subordinated to unrelated and unjustified political aggrievances of certain States, such as those related to economic sanctions. Pursuant to that view, the secretariat should be mandated to analyse how existing UNCITRAL texts can be best used to contribute to international and domestic climate actions and could also be used to "map" climate-related issues in additional areas of international trade law, with a view to presenting a narrowly tailored proposal at a later stage. Any specific proposal should clearly demonstrate why UNCITRAL would be the appropriate forum to address it. It would be particularly unhelpful for the Commission to venture into any area related to ongoing climate negotiations, in particular within the United Nations climate change regime (including UNFCCC), and that any work by UNCITRAL should remain within the confines of its expertise.

198. An intermediate view, which eventually gathered wide support, was that a mapping exercise beginning in the area of voluntary carbon credits, on which work was already under way at UNIDROIT, might represent a useful contribution by UNCITRAL to help States assess the options available to them in addressing relevant legal issues, some of which had already been identified in the secretariat's studies, in particular as regards the legal nature of voluntary carbon credits. Such analysis could also be helpful, for instance, to develop capacity of the private sector in implementation of projects consistent with article 6 of the Paris Agreement. It would be important, however, for such work to describe and analyse issues rather than to prescribe possible solutions or formulate models so as to avoid interference and duplication with the work of the competent bodies under existing international agreements in the area of climate change. Moreover, such work should be inclusive, in particular as regards the participation of experts representing Member States especially developing countries and should give competent government officials the opportunity to provide substantive input and information on their policies and practices. No formal consultative body needed to be created, nor would it be necessary for those experts to meet in person – albeit some had suggested an occasion for an in-person meeting might be provided in the context of UNCITRAL annual sessions – as long as all interested Member States had the opportunity to contribute to the work, including through questionnaires to be sent out by the secretariat. Bearing in mind diverging views and different concerns, the Commission decided on the future work in this regard as detailed in the next paragraph.

199. The Commission requested the secretariat, within the mandate of UNCITRAL, to consult with all Member States of the United Nations with a view to developing a more detailed study on the aspects of international trade law related to voluntary carbon credits. Such study should include consideration of outputs from other relevant

[67] United Nations, *Treaty Series*, vol. 1771, No. 30822.

forums and processes, including UNFCCC, and whether UNCITRAL efforts would be redundant. The secretariat should conduct such study in cooperation and collaboration with UNFCCC, UNIDROIT, HCCH and other organizations with relevant expertise. The secretariat should also invite all Member States of the United Nations to nominate experts to provide inputs to the work of the secretariat in this area. The secretariat was requested to aim for as wide representation as possible, in particular representation from developing countries. The Commission requested the secretariat to make the study available well in advance of its fifty-seventh session, and to provide an opportunity for all States Members of the United Nations to submit views and comments on the study. The Commission requested the secretariat to submit the study, as well as a compilation of the views and comments received from States, in advance of its fifty-seventh session.

4. Legal issues relating to the use of distributed ledger technology in trade

200. The Commission recalled that, at its fifty-fifth session, in 2022, it had requested the secretariat to prepare a guidance document on legal issues relating to the use of distributed ledger systems in trade, within existing resources, and in cooperation with other concerned organizations, as appropriate.[68] The Commission also recalled that the purpose of such a guidance document was to provide explanations useful to commercial operators, especially MSMEs and operators located in developing countries, in assessing whether distributed ledger technology-enabled services addressed their needs, and the impact of the use of such services on their business.[69] Raising awareness of those legal issues could also promote greater security and sustainability in digital transformation efforts, including within the United Nations system itself.[70]

201. At the present session, the Commission had before it a note by the Secretariat on legal issues relating to the use of distributed ledger technology in trade (scoping paper) (A/CN.9/1146). The Commission noted with appreciation the content of the scoping paper and highlighted its intersection with other digital trade workstreams of UNCITRAL such as the work carried out by Working Groups II, IV and V. It was indicated that the guidance document should focus on private law aspects of the use of distributed ledger technologies and address practical issues rather than theoretical ones. Broad support was expressed for the work to be carried out in close coordination with other concerned international organizations, and its relevance for several projects recently undertaken by HCCH was noted.

202. Noting the relevance of the guidance document also for the use of distributed ledger technology in the United Nations system, the Commission asked the secretariat to continue and finalize its work on the preparation of a guidance document on legal issues relating to the use of distributed ledger systems in trade, within existing resources, and in cooperation with other concerned organizations, as appropriate. The secretariat invited States and observers to share comments on the substance of the scoping paper as well as names of experts to be involved in the next steps of the project, with a view to ensuring balanced geographical representation and duly reflecting views of developing countries.

5. Dispute resolution in the digital economy

203. The Commission recalled that, at its fifty-fifth session, in 2022, it had requested the secretariat to continue to implement the stocktaking project on dispute resolution in the digital economy that was endorsed at its fifty-fourth session in 2021, and to report on the preliminary findings at its fifty-sixth session, in 2023.[71]

204. At the present session, the Commission had before it notes by the Secretariat on taxonomy and preliminary findings of the stocktaking of developments in dispute

[68] A/77/17, paras. 22 (f) and 169.
[69] A/77/17, para. 167.
[70] Ibid., para. 167.
[71] Ibid., para. 222.

resolution in the digital economy (A/CN.9/1154 and A/CN.9/1155). The Commission took note that, in response to its request, the notes by the Secretariat were prepared to: (a) identify, define and categorize new and conventional digital technologies and technology-enabled services and discuss their application to and impact on dispute resolution; (b) assess whether there are normative gaps in existing UNCITRAL texts and identify areas where there is a need to update or complement those texts or develop new ones; and (c) outline preliminary findings on the suggested way forward, including on possible future work. It was also informed that the Government of Japan, through its Ministry of Justice, contributed $377,537 for an additional period of 12 months to implement the stocktaking project. The Commission expressed its gratitude to the Government of Japan for its generous contribution and for its willingness to continue to support the project.

205. After a presentation by the secretariat on the implementation of the stocktaking project, the Commission first discussed the notes by the Secretariat generally, and secondly, focused on specific topics identified during the exploratory work.

206. General support was expressed on the approach and methodology that the secretariat had taken in implementing the stocktaking project, and it was widely felt that the project's implementation should continue along the same lines. It was mentioned that the project could already prioritize and focus on a few topics identified in the notes. It was nonetheless pointed out that not all of the project's activities had been completed, including activities for the "world tour", which still needed to cover more developing States. After discussion, it was generally felt that the secretariat should develop concrete work proposals for consideration by the Commission at its next session while further monitoring general developments in the area of "dispute resolution in the digital economy". The importance of looking into existing UNCITRAL texts on electronic commerce and coordinating with UNIDROIT and HCCH on certain topics was underscored. Furthermore, it was mentioned that experts on information technology should be consulted, where needed.

207. Additionally, it was mentioned that the enabling aspects of digitalization in dispute resolution had clear advantages, such as increased efficiency, but that unintended consequences of the use of new technology should be examined, such as biased decision-making. Moreover, it was mentioned that the requirement to use new technology could be costly for the parties to a dispute, in particular, the ongoing costs for maintenance and updating technology for businesses in developing countries. Reference was also made to the need to take into account digital literacy and culture.

208. On the recognition and enforcement of electronic awards, general support was expressed to further explore whether it was necessary to undertake work on a legal framework to overcome the obstacles to a broader acceptance of the issuance, service and enforcement of electronic awards. It was emphasized that legal uncertainties persisted even if parties agreed to, and institutional rules foresaw, the issuance of electronic awards. It was suggested that the secretariat should present legislative options in putting forward that topic as part of the future work.

209. Reference was made to article 20 of the United Nations Convention on the Use of Electronic Communications in International Contracts,[72] which applied to arbitration agreements. It was also discussed whether the New York Convention on the Recognition and Enforcement of Foreign Arbitral Awards (the "New York Convention")[73] needed to be amended or supplemented. In that regard, the secretariat was encouraged to consider the reasons that led the Commission not to consider possible amendments to the New York Convention when modernizing the requirements for the written form of the arbitration agreement in the UNCITRAL Model Law on International Commercial Arbitration with amendments as adopted in 2006,[74] as well as the special circumstances on which the Commission was able to rely in 2006 when adopting its Recommendation regarding the interpretation of

[72] United Nations publication, Sales No. E.07.V.2.

[73] United Nations, *Treaty Series*, vol. 330, No. 4739, p. 3.

[74] United Nations publication, Sales No. E.08.V.4.

article II, paragraph 2, and article VII, paragraph 1, of the New York Convention, which needed to be taken into account in the exploratory work. It was also said that deciding to amend the New York Convention could be interpreted as an implicit acknowledgement that the Convention in its current form was insufficient.

210. As for the topic of guidance on electronic notices of arbitration and their service, there were views expressed that it was an important issue to consider. Given the developments within different domestic jurisdictions, further exploratory work was suggested, in particular with reference to the work undertaken by HCCH in respect of electronical means to support the implementation of the Convention on the Service Abroad of Judicial and Extrajudicial Documents in Civil or Commercial Matters.[75] It was expressed that the possibilities of providing a legal framework for electronic notices of arbitration and their service should be looked into, and that a mere guidance text would not provide sufficient legal certainty. Issuing recommendations regarding the New York Convention in this aspect was also suggested. Furthermore, it was mentioned that article 2 of the UNCITRAL Arbitration Rules would be a useful model to address the issue of electronic notices and their service. If the notice of arbitration was delivered via email to a designated address pursuant to article 2 of the UNCITRAL Arbitration Rules, there would not be a lack of proper service resulting in an unenforceable award. Another view was that service by electronic means would provide a solution in circumstances where service by hand or by post was difficult.

211. Regarding the topic of e-document production, it was mentioned that it was highly controversial, and doubts about the added value of delving into that topic were raised. Another view was that e-document production was a common problem in international arbitration and that the secretariat should also consider whether the accepted limits on e-document production, such as those reflected in the IBA Rules on the Taking of Evidence in International Arbitration,[76] were being followed in most international arbitrations that were guided by these Rules.

212. On interim measures on the preservation of intangible property, it was mentioned that the current work undertaken by UNIDROIT and HCCH should be taken into account. While UNCITRAL Working Group V was currently undertaking work on asset tracing, it was said that such work was not conducted from an arbitration perspective.

213. With respect to dispute resolution on online platforms and on distributed ledger technology systems, there was support for further exploratory work especially on online platforms and for the secretariat to continue to collaborate with the Inclusive Global Legal Innovation Platform on Online Dispute Resolution. However, a diverging view was expressed which questioned the usefulness of exploring the use of online platforms, also in view of the previous work conducted by UNCITRAL on the Technical Notes on Online Dispute Resolution.

214. Regarding the use of artificial intelligence in international arbitration, it was generally acknowledged that the underlying technology was evolving rapidly. One view was that further monitoring and development would be needed, while others questioned the usefulness and suitability of UNCITRAL looking into that area.

215. In conclusion, the Commission noted with great appreciation the work carried out by the secretariat and the notes by the Secretariat on taxonomy and preliminary findings of stocktaking of developments in dispute resolution in the digital economy and, in light of the broad support expressed, requested the secretariat to continue to implement the stocktaking project, including the "world tour", to put forward proposals for possible legislative work with a focus on the topics on the recognition and enforcement of electronic awards and electronic notices of arbitration and their

[75] Convention of 15 November 1965 on the Service Abroad of Judicial and Extrajudicial Documents in Civil or Commercial Matters.

[76] IBA Rules on the Taking of Evidence in International Arbitration, adopted by a resolution of the IBA Council on 17 December 2020.

service, and to report on further progress made overall, taking into account the discussions which took place at the present session.

C. Working methods of UNCITRAL

216. The Commission recalled that, at its fifty-fifth session, in 2022, it had considered possible adjustments to its methods of work in light of the experience accumulated from the holding of UNCITRAL sessions during the COVID-19 pandemic.

217. Among other things, the Commission had agreed to continue to arrange for the meetings of its working groups to be made available on a streaming or videoconferencing platform, which would allow delegates participating remotely to listen to the deliberations but not make active interventions.[77] However, it had been stressed that any such arrangement should continue to promote inclusivity and should seek to be effective in relation to costs and budgets.[78]

218. At the present session, the Commission had before it a note by the Secretariat giving a general overview of the work programme of the Commission and of its working groups and its secretariat, including methods of work (A/CN.9/1140). The Commission noted that the Secretariat had provided live streaming of all sessions of the working groups since the fifty-fifth session of the Commission, as well as the present session of the Commission, in the six official languages of the United Nations (although without the possibility for remote participants to make interventions). The Commission was informed that the secretariat had incurred costs for the livestreaming of the sessions, which was currently not included in the regular budget of UNCITRAL and its secretariat. In that context, there was strong support for continuing to livestream the sessions, as it would allow for inclusiveness and transparency and lead to broader participation by subject-matter experts in real time. While support was also expressed for a hybrid interactive format of UNCITRAL sessions, it was stated that this would limit the conference time allocated to the sessions and might create difficulties for some delegates to obtain approval to attend sessions in person. After discussion, the Commission requested the secretariat to seek ways to continue the livestreaming of UNCITRAL sessions within the existing resources of the Secretariat.

219. With regard to the use of the final meetings of the working group session to continue substantive deliberations, the Commission confirmed that Working Group III (or any other working group, when the need arose) could continue to use the final meetings of its sessions for substantive deliberations, and adopt the report of the session by a written procedure.

220. A proposal with two options was put forward to guide the secretariat when organizing informal meetings of working groups in between formal sessions. One option was that the working groups should decide how and when intersessional informal meetings could be organized and set the agenda. The other option was that the Commission should invite the working groups to discuss how intersessional informal work can best be organized, and to set the agenda. At the outset, it was clarified that the proposal did not aim to address the methods of work by Working Group III, which had already been agreed by the Working Group, nor address the expert meetings organized by the secretariat. Some concerns were expressed about organizing informal meetings (including in respect of intersessional meetings of Working Group III), as some delegates might not be able to participate due to limited time and resources as well as the lack of interpretation. There was, however, broad support for organizing informal meetings so as to enhance the efficiency and productivity of deliberations during the formal sessions. It was noted that such informal meetings should not be used to take decisions for, or pre-empt or foreclose the decisions by, a working group and that the number of informal consultations

[77] A/77/17, para. 237.

[78] Ibid.

should not be excessive, as that could limit the participation of certain delegations. The importance of ensuring that delegations had equal opportunity to take part in informal meetings in light of the different time zones involved was emphasized. It was added that the organization of such meetings should not have any impact on the regular budget of UNCITRAL and its secretariat. A suggestion was made for the recordings of informal meetings to be made available to all delegates of the working group.

221. After deliberations, the Commission agreed that each working group should decide how and when informal meetings of the working group would be organized by the secretariat in between its sessions. The Commission further agreed that the agenda of such meetings should be agreed by the working group and announced in advance in order to facilitate the participation of the delegates involved. The Commission noted that in that process, the working groups and the secretariat should ensure (a) the inclusiveness and transparency of the informal meetings, (b) that no decision would be taken during informal meetings, (c) that an excessive burden would not be put on delegates to attend such meetings, (d) that recordings of the meetings were made available to delegates who could not attend, and (e) that interpretation would be provided to the extent possible and resources permitting.

222. In respect of holding informal meetings during the Commission session, the Commission agreed to continue its practice of informal meetings during the formal sessions.

XIII. Coordination and cooperation

A. General

223. The Commission had before it a note by the Secretariat (A/CN.9/1143) providing information on the activities of international organizations in the field of international trade law in which the secretariat had participated since the fifty-fifth session of the Commission. The Commission thanked the secretariat for its efforts to follow closely the work of other organizations and to cooperate and coordinate with them in the implementation of its own and those other organizations' work programmes, in particular UNIDROIT and HCCH.

224. The Commission noted with appreciation the cooperation between its secretariat and UNIDROIT in the preparation of a model law on warehouse receipts (see chap. XII, sect. B.1, and A/CN.9/1152). The Commission also took note of the cooperation between the secretariat and UNIDROIT in the area of factoring, as well as the general coordination of their work in the area of secured transactions, and noted further the cooperation on various other UNIDROIT projects, including the working group on digital assets and private law, the working group on best practices for effective enforcement, the working group on bank insolvency and the working group on the legal structure of agricultural enterprises. The Commission noted the constraints faced by its secretariat in following those various working groups in addition to its support to the Commission's own work programme and expressed its appreciation to UNIDROIT for its willingness to incorporate the contributions of the UNCITRAL secretariat during its deliberations and in any event before finalizing those instruments as UNIDROIT texts. As regards HCCH, the Commission took note with appreciation of the continued interest of the HCCH secretariat in the development of a taxonomy of legal issues related to the digital economy and in the area of applicable law in insolvency proceedings and civil asset tracing and recovery.[79]

225. The Commission noted with appreciation that the UNCITRAL secretariat had been invited as member to meetings of the World Bank Group ICR Task Force that

[79] See the draft agenda for the meeting of the HCCH Council on General Affairs and Policy held from 7 to 10 March 2023 (CGAP 2023) (available at https://hcch.net).

assisted the World Bank Group to regularly test and evaluate the effectiveness and relevance of the ICR Principles, ensuring the standard was disseminated and global consensus maintained in close partnership with UNCITRAL. The Commission stressed the importance of ensuring coherence between the work of UNCITRAL and that of the World Bank Group on that matter.

226. More generally, the Commission expressed its satisfaction for the efforts made by the secretariat to cooperate and coordinate work with other organizations and entities, within and outside the United Nations system, both at a general level and on specific topics of the Commission's work programme, including Asia-Pacific Economic Cooperation, the Economic and Monetary Community of Central Africa, the Inter-Agency Task Force on Financing for Development, the International Centre for Settlement of Investment Disputes, the International Federation of Freight Forwarders Associations, the Intergovernmental Organisation for International Carriage by Rail, OECD, PCA, the Economic Commission for Europe, the Economic and Social Commission for Asia and the Pacific, the World Bank and the World Trade Organization.

227. The Commission reiterated the importance of coordinating the activities of organizations active in the field of international trade law, which was a core element of the mandate that UNCITRAL received from the General Assembly,[80] as a means of avoiding duplication of efforts and promoting efficiency, consistency and coherence in the unification and harmonization of international trade law. The Commission noted instances where the secretariats of UNCITRAL, UNIDROIT and HCCH had faced difficulties to coordinate their work. The Commission also noted the difficulties faced by member States to follow various initiatives and the risk of scheduling conflicts among meetings of different organizations. The Commission welcomed the commitment of the secretariats to continue working closely to achieve greater coordination and to engage in a closer cooperative dialogue in framing their respective work programmes, agendas, dates of meetings and timelines in order to ensure an efficient deployment of the resources of member States. In that connection, the Commission welcomed the initiative of the secretariats of UNCITRAL, UNIDROIT and HCCH to develop joint terms of reference to facilitate and strengthen the cooperation and coordination between the three organizations, in particular as regards the adoption of future work, in order to avoid overlap between work programmes and to avoid possible risks of inconsistency; and to implement procedures to better coordinate operational processes between the three organizations. The Commission looked forward to being appraised of those terms of reference once they were finalized. The Commission also encouraged the secretariats of the three organizations to share information about their planned activities with member States regularly, bearing in mind their respective memberships, governance structures and working methods.

B. Reports of other international organizations

228. The Commission took note of the statements made on behalf of international and regional organizations invited to the session, which focused on activities of relevance for UNCITRAL.

1. Hague Conference on Private International Law

229. The Commission heard a statement by the Deputy Secretary-General of HCCH setting out areas of continued cooperation of HCCH with UNCITRAL, noting, in particular:

(a) The cooperation between HCCH, UNIDROIT and UNCITRAL on legal issues arising from digital economy, in particular the taxonomy and the UNIDROIT

[80] See General Assembly resolution 2205 (XXI), sect. II, para. 8.

project on digital assets, as well as on applicable law in insolvency proceedings and civil asset tracing and recovery;

(b) The HCCH Permanent Bureau had participated as an observer of UNCITRAL Working Group V and continued to hold a mandate from its Council on General Affairs and Policy to monitor developments with respect to the law applicable to insolvency proceedings, including issues relating to the treatment of digital transactions and digital assets in insolvency proceedings. The Permanent Bureau looked forward to continuing the discussions on the types of rules of private international law that were envisaged in that project, and to identifying when this examination would require the input of the Permanent Bureau, potentially in a joint initiative with UNCITRAL; and

(c) The Permanent Bureau was grateful to the UNCITRAL secretariat for having contributed to the Conference on Commercial, Digital and Financial Law Across Borders (CODIFI), held in September 2022, and the Permanent Bureau, in turn, participated as an observer in UNCITRAL Working Group IV, holding a mandate under its digital economy project to continue monitoring developments with respect to artificial intelligence, digital platforms and automated contracting, in partnership with subject-matter experts and with UNCITRAL. While the primary matters under examination in Working Group IV concerned the substantive law of contracting, attribution and liability, the general topics of artificial intelligence and automation were of importance to the Permanent Bureau as they had implications for continuing work on matters related to cross-border use of distributed ledger technology and the topic of technology neutrality.

2. UNIDROIT

230. The Secretary-General of UNIDROIT reported on the developments concerning several UNIDROIT activities. The Commission was informed, in particular, about the following:

(a) At its 102nd session (Rome, 10–12 May 2023), the UNIDROIT Governing Council took note of the progress made since its 101st session on the joint UNCITRAL/UNIDROIT model law on warehouse receipts project, as well as of the proposed next steps concerning the drafting of a guide to enactment to that model law. The Council unanimously adopted the final version of the draft model law on warehouse receipts, agreeing that it was ready for submission to UNCITRAL for State negotiations and completion;

(b) At the same session, the UNIDROIT Governing Council also adopted the UNIDROIT Model Law on Factoring. That project as well had greatly benefited from the excellent cooperation between UNIDROIT and the UNCITRAL secretariat;

(c) At that session, the UNIDROIT Governing Council also approved the UNIDROIT Principles on Digital Assets and Private Law. The UNCITRAL secretariat had participated at the sixth session (in hybrid format, 31 August–2 September 2022), seventh session (in hybrid format, 19–21 December 2022), eighth session (in hybrid format, 8–10 March 2023) and ninth session (online, 5 April 2023) of the corresponding UNIDROIT working group, and the final version approved by the UNIDROIT Governing Council reflected several comments made by the UNCITRAL secretariat, which contributed to refining the final text and for which UNIDROIT was grateful; and

(d) UNIDROIT work on best practices for effective enforcement, bank insolvency and the legal structure of agricultural enterprises also proceeded, and UNIDROIT welcomed the input of UNCITRAL in those areas as well.

3. Permanent Court of Arbitration

231. The representative of PCA made a statement providing an overview of the experience of PCA in 2022 with the UNCITRAL Arbitration Rules and addressing its cooperation with Working Groups II and III. The Commission was informed of the

experience of PCA in providing registry services to international arbitrations conducted under the UNCITRAL Arbitration Rules (including the 1976, 2010, 2013 and 2021 versions) and the role of the Secretary-General of PCA as designating authority or appointing authority under these Rules (including the review of arbitrator fees). The Commission noted that the UNCITRAL Rules on Transparency in Treaty-based Investor-State Arbitration were not applicable in any of the investor-State cases commenced at PCA in 2022. The Commission took note with satisfaction of the contributions made by PCA to the work of Working Groups II and III, in particular with respect to the UNCITRAL Code of Conduct for Arbitrators in International Investment Dispute Resolution adopted by the Commission at the present session (see para. 90 above and annex III).

C. International governmental and non-governmental organizations invited to sessions of UNCITRAL and its working groups

232. At its present session, the Commission considered a note by the Secretariat (A/CN.9/1142) presenting information about international governmental and non-governmental organizations invited to sessions of UNCITRAL and its working groups. The note had been prepared in line with the request of the Commission, at its fiftieth session, in 2017, that the secretariat should provide such information in writing for future sessions.[81] The Commission took note of the newly accepted non-governmental organizations, the non-governmental organizations whose applications had been declined since the fifty-fifth session of the Commission, in 2022, as well as of updates on the separate list of additional non-governmental organizations invited only to sessions of Working Group III while it was working on issues of investor-State dispute settlement reform.

XIV. Technical assistance to law reform

A. General

233. The Commission had before it the following notes by the Secretariat, addressing activities undertaken to support the adoption, use and uniform interpretation of UNCITRAL texts ("non-legislative activities"), in the following areas: technical cooperation and assistance (A/CN.9/1138); activities of the UNCITRAL Regional Centre for Asia and the Pacific (A/CN.9/1137); and the dissemination of information and related activities to support the work of UNCITRAL and the use of its texts, including reports on CLOUT and digests of case law (A/CN.9/1139). The Commission noted that the notes covered activities from 1 April 2022 to 31 March 2023 (the "reporting period").

234. The Commission recalled that non-legislative activities included raising awareness and promoting the effective understanding of UNCITRAL texts; providing legislative advice and assistance to States for the adoption and use of those texts; and outreach and capacity-building to support their effective use, implementation and uniform interpretation.

B. Technical cooperation and assistance and capacity-building activities

1. Overall cooperation, including cooperation pursuant to formal agreements with governments

235. The Commission expressed its appreciation for the continued efforts made by the secretariat to meet the increasing demand for non-legislative activities, including

[81] A/72/17, para. 364.

the focus on beneficiary countries with lower levels of development, as well as the continued focus on engaging with countries from Latin America and the Caribbean and from Africa. The Commission noted that, while more activities could be undertaken in person due to the easing or lifting of COVID-19 measures, the secretariat had continued to hold and participate in numerous activities remotely, to sustain its level of engagement given the limited available resources.

236. The Commission welcomed in particular the milestones reached in the implementation of formal agreements with governments (namely with the Government of Singapore; the Ministry of Commerce of China; the Department of Justice of the government of Hong Kong, China; and the Ministry of Commerce and the National Competitiveness Center of Saudi Arabia), and in its other cooperation frameworks with partner organizations and institutions.

2. UNCITRAL Days

237. The Commission welcomed the continued expansion of the secretariat's engagement with academic partners, geared towards students, young researchers and practitioners in international trade law, through the UNCITRAL Days series in Asia and the Pacific (since 2014), in Latin America and the Caribbean (since 2020), and, for the first time, in Africa, in 2022.

238. The Commission welcomed the fact that the inaugural series of UNCITRAL Days in Africa took stock of the entry into force in May 2019 of the Agreement Establishing the African Continental Free Trade Area, and that the focus of the UNCITRAL Latin America and Caribbean Days 2022 was on MSMEs. The Commission further noted that the UNCITRAL Asia-Pacific Days in 2022 celebrated the 10th anniversary of the Regional Centre for Asia and the Pacific and explored how legal harmonization through the work of UNCITRAL could benefit both traditional and new areas of trade in the Asia and Pacific region in the coming decade.

239. The Commission noted that the reports on the 2022 UNCITRAL Days were available on the UNCITRAL website. It extended its congratulations to all participants and hosts of the UNCITRAL Days in 2022. The Commission looked forward to institutions from additional countries and jurisdictions taking part in events for the 2023 edition, and it encouraged the secretariat to maintain the high quality of the series while welcoming the indication that similar events might be planned also in the future for West Asia.

3. Activities across thematic areas

240. The Commission congratulated the secretariat for the continuation of its intensive engagement in capacity-building, and technical and cooperation efforts across all thematic areas, as evidenced in document A/CN.9/1138.

241. In particular, regarding insolvency, the Commission welcomed the secretariat's initiatives and the coordination with other stakeholders towards the celebration of the twenty-fifth anniversary of the UNCITRAL Model Law on Cross-Border Insolvency. The Commission further welcomed the secretariat's continued collaboration with, among others, the World Bank Group, the International Insolvency Institute and INSOL International in insolvency-related capacity-building and outreach events. The Commission encouraged the secretariat to continue such collaborations and noted that they might lead to creating new opportunities for legislative assistance and support, in particular with regard to developing countries.

242. Further, regarding electronic commerce, the Commission welcomed the cooperation of the secretariat with the International Chamber of Commerce Digital Standards Initiative, the Asian Development Bank, the Economic and Social Commission for Asia and the Pacific and the United Nations Conference on Trade and Development, and other concerned entities, to promote the adoption of the Model Law on Electronic Transferable Records and other relevant UNCITRAL texts in response

to demands from stakeholders, to overcome the effects of trade disruption due to exceptional events and to promote efficient and paperless trade flows.

243. With regard to dispute resolution, the Commission recognized the increasing number of technical assistance and related activities arising from a broad range of different means of dispute resolution (arbitration, mediation, investor-State dispute settlement) and the number of different legal texts prepared by the Commission on such means. The Commission noted the importance of providing an overview of the different means and how they interrelated, including the availability of different instruments for different stakeholders, such as States, arbitration and mediation institutions, as well as contractual and disputing parties. It was further noted that with the adoption of texts relating to investor-State dispute settlement, it might be necessary to elaborate how UNCITRAL texts operated in the respective context. The Commission expressed its appreciation to the secretariat for furthering the universal application of the New York Convention and for the increased number of accessions and ratifications to the United Nations Convention on International Settlement Agreements Resulting from Mediation. The Commission noted the increased integration of the non-legislative activities led by the secretariat with the ongoing legislative work in various areas to enhance participation in its legislative activities.

C. Dissemination of information on the work and texts of UNCITRAL

1. Website, social media and other outreach activities

244. The Commission welcomed the secretariat's continued efforts in expanding its online presence through its website (https://uncitral.un.org), and through social media platforms such as YouTube, LinkedIn, Facebook and X (formerly Twitter), as well as its other outreach activities reported in a note by the Secretariat (A/CN.9/1139). With regard to the use of social media as an entry point to the work of UNCITRAL, the Commission recalled that the General Assembly had welcomed the use of social media in accordance with the applicable guidelines.[82]

245. The Commission welcomed the comprehensive statistics on the usage of the website, especially those showing its significance as a multilingual source of information on international trade law. Recalling the General Assembly resolutions commending the website's six-language interface, the Commission commended the secretariat for its continued efforts to provide, through the website, UNCITRAL texts, publications and related information in a timely manner and in the six official languages of the United Nations.

246. The Commission also expressed its thanks to the UNOV/UNODC Information Technology Service and the Office of Information and Communications Technology for providing the secretariat with the necessary technical support to carry out its mandate, including in relation to the secretariat initiatives for the implementation of a new planning and reporting tool for its activities, to upgrade and incorporate new tools on the Commission website and to upgrade the CLOUT online database as part of the rejuvenation of CLOUT (see paras. 270 and 271 below).

247. The Commission heard a proposal to better orient the presentation of its work products towards end users. It was proposed that the current presentation of texts on the website, organized by topic and working groups, could be complemented by a presentation more oriented towards users, for example, MSMEs, to facilitate their access to UNCITRAL texts. It was also proposed that each working group should be invited, before the completion of its texts, to consider to whom their texts might be useful and how that target audience could be reached. Those proposals received support, and the secretariat was invited to take them into account as far as possible when presenting the texts on the Internet and in its exchanges with working groups.

[82] For more information, see A/77/17, paras. 264 and 267.

2. UNCITRAL Law Library

248. The Commission emphasized the important role played by the UNCITRAL Law Library, especially its provision of online services and timely responses to information requests.

3. International commercial law moot competitions

249. The Commission commended the secretariat for its continued co-sponsoring of major international commercial law moot competitions. It noted with interest the information provided on the Willem C. Vis International Commercial Arbitration Moot ("Vis Moot"), and on all the moot competitions which the secretariat had supported and participated in, including those organized in Arabic and Spanish, mentioned in paragraphs 53–63 of a note by the Secretariat (A/CN.9/1139).

4. UNCITRAL e-learning programme

250. The Commission congratulated the secretariat on making three new e-learning modules available to government officials, UNCITRAL delegates and prospective delegates and users of UNCITRAL texts generally. It was noted that the three new e-learning modules covered mediation, public procurement and public-private partnerships, and commercial arbitration, bringing the total to four courses and a total of six modules.[83] The Commission acknowledged the secretariat's partnership with the Ministry of Commerce of China and the International Training Centre of the International Labour Organization in that regard. The Commission encouraged the secretariat to further increase the number of e-learning modules on UNCITRAL instruments and its work, and it noted the importance of the e-learning programme in terms of the outreach and the capacity-building mandates of the Commission. Noting the need for additional resources in that area, the Commission expressed its hope that support would be provided by member States and relevant organizations towards the development of further UNCITRAL e-learning modules and the translation of available and future modules in the six official languages of the United Nations.

5. Future activities

251. The Commission welcomed the information highlighting activities planned from April 2023 onwards, as a planning tool for States and other potential participants. The Commission noted in particular the signing ceremony for the United Nations Convention on the International Effects of Judicial Sales of Ships.[84] It invited all member States to attend the signing ceremony, which would be held in Beijing on 5 September 2023, and to consider signing or otherwise acceding to the Convention.

6. General assessment of the outreach and capacity-building activities of the secretariat

252. The Commission noted that the whole range of outreach and capacity-building activities led by the secretariat, including through its online and social media presence, continued to generate increasing interest in UNCITRAL among a broad audience, including some that had not previously engaged with UNCITRAL. The Commission encouraged the secretariat to continue all those efforts.

[83] The first course was made available in July 2021 and consists of an introduction to UNCITRAL in three modules (introduction to harmonized commercial law and its relevance for economic development; origin, organization and methods of work of UNCITRAL; and the contribution of UNCITRAL to sustainable development).

[84] United Nations publication, Sales No. E.23.V.7.

D. Resources and funding

1. Voluntary contributions to UNCITRAL trust funds

253. The Commission recalled the need for extrabudgetary funds to meet the costs of non-legislative activities and welcomed the secretariat's ongoing efforts to secure voluntary contributions to the UNCITRAL trust funds and for the operation and promotion of the Transparency Registry (see para. 287 below).

254. Requesting that the secretariat pursue these efforts, the Commission recalled its previous statements on the importance of efficiency in the delivery of non-legislative activities and the need for the secretariat to remain neutral and independent in collaborative delivery.[85]

2. Trust fund for symposiums

255. The Commission expressed its gratitude to the member States and organizations that had contributed to the UNCITRAL trust fund for symposiums since the Commission's fifty-fifth session, in particular:

(a) To the Government of China, under a memorandum of understanding with the United Nations;

(b) To the Government of France, under a grant agreement to support research on investor-State dispute settlement reform, interpretation and travel;

(c) To the Government of Japan, under a memorandum of understanding with the United Nations in support of stocktaking of developments in dispute resolution in the digital economy;

(d) To the Government of Saudi Arabia, under a memorandum of understanding with the United Nations.

256. The Commission noted that, despite active fundraising by the secretariat, the balances in the trust funds remained insufficient to meet the anticipated demand for non-legislative activities and requests for travel assistance. The Commission accordingly reiterated its call to all States, international organizations and other interested entities to consider making contributions to the UNCITRAL trust fund for symposiums, preferably in the form of multi-year contributions or as specific-purpose contributions, to facilitate planning and enable the secretariat to meet the increasing number of requests for these activities.

3. Trust fund established to provide travel assistance to developing countries that are members of UNCITRAL

257. The Commission noted that a single contribution was received since the fifty-fifth session for the trust fund established to provide travel assistance to developing countries that are members of UNCITRAL. The Commission accordingly appealed to the relevant bodies of the United Nations system and to all organizations, institutions and individuals to make contributions to that trust fund. The Commission expressed its appreciation to the Government of Austria for its contribution.

258. The Commission further expressed its appreciation to the European Union and the Swiss Agency for Development and Cooperation whose respective multi-year contributions, earmarked specifically for the participation of delegates and observers of developing countries in sessions related to the work of Working Group III on investor-State dispute settlement reform, facilitated the participation of delegates and observers from Algeria, Argentina, Armenia, Benin, Burkina Faso, Chad, Côte d'Ivoire, the Democratic Republic of the Congo, Ecuador, Gabon, Haiti, Iran (Islamic Republic of), Jamaica, Lesotho, Mauritius, Pakistan, Panama, Sierra Leone, Tunisia,

[85] See, for instance, A/73/17, para. 188; and A/77/17, para. 273.

Uganda and Zimbabwe in the sessions of Working Group that had taken place during the reporting period.

4. Voluntary contributions towards the operation and the promotion of the Transparency Registry

259. The Commission acknowledged, with gratitude, the contributions and support from the European Commission, the Organization of the Petroleum Exporting Countries (OPEC) Fund for International Development and the Federal Ministry for Economic Cooperation and Development (BMZ) of Germany for the operation of the Transparency Registry, and for promoting the UNCITRAL transparency standards.[86] The Commission called for additional contributions and appealed to the relevant bodies of the United Nations system and to all organizations, institutions and individuals to make contributions for those purposes, in order to allow the secretariat to continue in its efforts in operating and promoting the Transparency Registry beyond June 2024, subject to the current mandate being extended beyond December 2023 by the General Assembly (see chap. XVI, sect. B below.)

E. Internship programme

260. The Commission welcomed the continuation of the UNCITRAL internship programme in Vienna and Incheon, Republic of Korea, and the information that remote internships remained a tool which could help broaden access to the internship programme by other regional groups and enhance linguistic and geographical diversity. The Commission reiterated its call to States and observer organizations to bring the possibility of an internship at UNCITRAL to the attention of interested persons and to consider granting scholarships for the purpose of attracting the most qualified candidates.

F. UNCITRAL presence in the Asia-Pacific region

261. The Commission recognized the important benefits for the Asia and Pacific region of its Regional Centre for Asia and the Pacific, which had continued to enhance the levels of awareness, adoption and implementation of UNCITRAL texts in the region.

262. The Commission noted the impact of the activities of the Regional Centre in the region, for example, the accessions by Turkmenistan and Timor-Leste to the New York Convention; the accession by Turkmenistan to the United Nations Convention on Contracts for the International Sale of Goods, and the extension of the territorial application of that Convention to Hong Kong, China; the ratification by the Philippines of, and the accession of Tuvalu to, the United Nations Convention on the Use of Electronic Communications in International Contracts; and the ratification by Kazakhstan of the United Nations Convention on International Settlement Agreements Resulting from Mediation. (For other treaty actions and enactments, see also chapter XVI below.) In addition, the Commission commended the active engagement by the Regional Centre with least developed countries, landlocked developing countries and small island developing States of the region, with 17 jurisdictions co-hosting or participating in activities carried out by the Regional Centre.[87]

263. The Commission also commended the Regional Centre for resuming in-person flagship activities as the region reopened after the pandemic while continuing to

---

[86] The Rules on Transparency in Treaty-based Investor-State Arbitration and the United Nations Convention on Transparency in Treaty-based Investor-State Arbitration, together with the transparency repository, are referred to as "the transparency standards".

[87] Namely, Afghanistan, Bangladesh, Bhutan, Cambodia, Fiji, Kazakhstan, Kyrgyzstan, Lao People's Democratic Republic, Maldives, Mongolia, Myanmar, Nepal, Solomon Islands, Timor-Leste, Turkmenistan, Tuvalu and Yemen.

expand their reach and accessibility through online or hybrid means to the extent possible during the reporting period, namely the eleventh edition of the Asia Pacific ADR Conference including the UNCITRAL ADR Special Session, and the RCAP@10 Conference, which all took place in Seoul in November 2022, and the ninth edition of the UNCITRAL Asia-Pacific Days. Regarding the latter, the Commission welcomed 16 events co-hosted with 28 partnering universities and institutions across nine jurisdictions in the region which, as in previous years, had proved highly successful in support of the activities and objectives of the Regional Centre.[88]

264. The Commission noted with appreciation the additional events and public, private and civil society initiatives that the Regional Centre had organized or supported through participation by the secretariat, and the technical assistance and capacity-building services provided to States, international and regional organizations and development banks in the region, noting the activities carried out had resulted in broader and deeper stakeholder engagement in the region and beyond. The Commission welcomed statements by Australia and Indonesia commending the work of the Regional Centre, and by the Republic of Korea expressing continued support and inviting other delegations to participate in the various in-person and hybrid activities spearheaded by the Regional Centre to promote legal certainty in international commercial transactions in Asia and the Pacific.

265. The Commission also expressed strong support for the Regional Centre's continued coordination and cooperation efforts with regional stakeholders, development banks and other institutions active in trade law reform, and with United Nations funds, programmes and specialized agencies active in the region.

266. The Commission noted that the Regional Centre was staffed with one professional-level staff member, one programme assistant, one team assistant and two legal experts secondees; that its core project budget allowed for the occasional employment of experts and consultants; and that, during the reporting period, the Regional Centre had received 21 interns. The Commission also noted that the Regional Centre relied fully on the annual financial contribution from the Incheon Metropolitan City to the UNCITRAL trust fund for symposiums to meet the cost of its operation and programme ($500,000 from 2011 to 2016 and $450,000 from 2017 to 2026).

267. The Commission expressed its gratitude to the City of Incheon and also expressed its gratitude to the Ministry of Justice of the Republic of Korea and to the government of the Hong Kong, China, for the extension of their contribution of two legal experts on non-reimbursable loans.

268. The Commission encouraged the secretariat to continue to seek cooperation, including through formal agreements, to ensure coordination and funding for the technical assistance and capacity-building activities of the Regional Centre. The Commission further repeated its call upon all States, international organizations and other interested entities to consider making contributions to the UNCITRAL trust funds to enable the continued delivery of those activities.

XV. Promotion of ways and means of ensuring a uniform interpretation and application of UNCITRAL legal texts

A. Case Law on UNCITRAL Texts

269. The Commission recalled the importance of the Case Law on UNCITRAL Texts (CLOUT) system, including digests of case law, in promoting the uniform interpretation of UNCITRAL texts. It welcomed the information on the seven CLOUT issues published in the period 2022–2023, comprising 71 abstracts of cases from 26 jurisdictions, and the information concerning the pattern of contributions to, and

[88] See also, UNCITRAL "Asia–Pacific Days report 2022".

use of, the CLOUT system comprising the online database. The Commission further welcomed the fact that cases from Armenia, Bahamas, Costa Rica and Saudi Arabia were added to the CLOUT online database for the first time.

270. The Commission noted with interest the progress achieved in the reporting period towards the rejuvenation of the CLOUT system, and it welcomed the initiatives of the secretariat as identified in paragraphs 33 and 36 of a note by the Secretariat (A/CN.9/1139), to build a more active and productive network of contributors to CLOUT, covering an expanded range of UNCITRAL texts (the "CLOUT Network"). Among the developments highlighted in the note by the Secretariat, the Commission welcomed the signing of new CLOUT Network institutional partnerships.

271. The Commission requested the secretariat to continue those rejuvenation efforts and reiterated its previous calls[89] for contributions from all legal traditions to its uniform interpretation tools, from voluntary contributors, institutional partners and national correspondents, and paying special attention to developing countries.

272. The Commission expressed its thanks to all States, organizations, institutions and individuals that contributed to CLOUT, whether as individual or institutional contributors, and appealed to all States and stakeholders to remain or become active contributors to the CLOUT Network.

273. The Commission further welcomed the information that, as of 31 March 2023, the secretariat had received 126 designations of CLOUT national correspondents from 53 Member States. Recalling its agreement to the establishment of the Steering Committee for CLOUT[90] the Commission expressed its thanks to the 13 Member States that have since designated a national correspondent to also serve as members of the Steering Committee for the same period as the term for national correspondents, that is, from 27 June 2022 through the last day prior to the beginning of the sixtieth Commission session, in 2027.

274. The Commission recalled that the role of the CLOUT Steering Committee was to provide support and encouragement to the CLOUT Network, through such activities as reporting on case law databases and sources of information relevant to CLOUT, raising awareness of CLOUT in all regions, monitoring the pattern of CLOUT contributions, making recommendations towards ensuring that CLOUT cases reflect the adoption and use of UNCITRAL texts in different legal systems and across all regions, and encouraging an expanded scope of UNCITRAL texts covered.

275. The Commission also noted the annual meeting of the CLOUT Network, comprising members of the Steering Committee, held on 31 March 2023 on the margins of the Vis Moot (see para. 249 above), in which the rejuvenation efforts were discussed. In particular, participants in the meeting discussed the possible ways to improve the electronic dissemination of CLOUT and to modernize the design and format of CLOUT issues in anticipation of a migration to a new, upgraded CLOUT platform.

276. In this regard, the Commission invited the secretariat to further advance the technical aspects of the rejuvenation efforts, both in regard to an upgrade to the CLOUT online database and to the possible sharing of CLOUT data with relevant third-party legal service providers, taking into account the parameters set forth in paragraph 38 of a note by the Secretariat (A/CN.9/1139).

277. Noting that the upgrade of the CLOUT online database would have budgetary implications, the Commission called upon the secretariat to identify additional resources which would enable the upgrade and migration.

278. In the case that resources could not be made available, the Commission called upon States, organizations, institutions and individuals to consider making

[89] A/77/17, para. 288.

[90] A/74/17, paras. 239–244.

contributions to the UNCITRAL trust fund for symposiums for the purpose of upgrading the CLOUT online database.

279. The Commission additionally requested the Office of Information and Communications Technology and the Information Technology Service, as applicable, to provide the support needed.

B. Digests and additional capacity-building materials

280. The Commission welcomed the indication that the secretariat was in the process of preparing a new edition of the *UNCITRAL 2012 Digest of Case Law on the Model Law on International Commercial Arbitration* and requested the secretariat to report on the progress of that initiative.

281. The Commission further noted the completion of the preparation of the updated version of the *UNCITRAL Model Law on Cross-Border Insolvency: The Judicial Perspective* further to its approval of the revised text at its fifty-fifth session.

C. 1958 New York Convention Guide website

282. The Commission took note with satisfaction of the continued growth of the 1958 New York Convention Guide website (www.newyorkconvention1958.org) and of the successful coordination between that website and the CLOUT system.

XVI. Status of conventions and model laws and the operation of the Transparency Registry

A. General discussion

283. The Commission considered the status of the conventions and model laws emanating from its work and the status of the New York Convention,[91] on the basis of a note by the Secretariat (A/CN.9/1136). The Commission noted with appreciation the information on treaty actions and legislative enactments received since its fifty-fifth session.

284. Several member States shared information on progress towards adoption of UNCITRAL texts, namely the United Nations Convention on International Settlement Agreements Resulting from Mediation[92] and other texts on alternative dispute resolution, the UNCITRAL Model Law on Electronic Transferable Records, including in the framework of the relevant Group of Seven declarations[93] and with the support of the ICC Digital Standards Initiative,[94] and the UNCITRAL Model Law on the Use and Cross-border Recognition of Identity Management and Trust Services (2022).[95]

285. The Commission also noted the following actions and legislative enactments made known to the UNCITRAL secretariat subsequent to the submission of the above-mentioned note:

(a) UNCITRAL Model Law on International Commercial Arbitration (1985) with amendments as adopted in 2006. Legislation based on the Model Law had been adopted in 87 States in a total of 120 jurisdictions. New legislation based on the Model Law has been adopted in Greece (2023), Japan (2023) and Sierra Leone (2022);

---

[91] United Nations, *Treaty Series*, vol. 330, No. 4739, p. 3.

[92] A/73/17, annex I.

[93] Group of Seven, Ministerial Declaration and annexes, of G7 Digital and Technology Ministers' meeting of 28 April 2021, and Group of Seven, Ministerial declaration of the G7 Digital Ministers' meeting of 11 May 2022.

[94] www.dsi.iccwbo.org/.

[95] United Nations publication, forthcoming.

(b) United Nations Convention on International Settlement Agreements Resulting from Mediation (New York, 2018).[96] Signature by the United Kingdom (2023) (10 States parties);

(c) UNCITRAL Model Law on Cross-Border Insolvency (1997). Legislation based on the Model Law had been adopted in 58 States in a total of 61 jurisdictions. New legislation based on the Model Law had been adopted in Albania (2016).

286. The Commission expressed appreciation to the General Assembly for the support it provided to UNCITRAL in its activities and in performing its distinct role in furthering the dissemination of international commercial law. In particular, the Commission referred to the long-established practice of the General Assembly, upon acting on UNCITRAL texts, to recommend to States to give favourable consideration to UNCITRAL texts and to request the Secretary-General to publish UNCITRAL texts, including electronically, in the six official languages of the United Nations, and take other measures to disseminate UNCITRAL texts as broadly as possible to Governments and all other relevant stakeholders.

B. Operation of the Transparency Registry and consideration of the way forward

287. The Commission recalled that article 8 of the UNCITRAL Rules on Transparency in Treaty-based Investor State Arbitration ("the Rules on Transparency") envisaged the establishment of a repository of published information (the "Transparency Registry") under the Rules on Transparency.[97] It was noted that the UNCITRAL secretariat had operated the Transparency Registry as a project funded entirely with voluntary contributions from the European Union, the OPEC Fund for International Development and BMZ since 2016.[98] The Commission further recalled the request by the General Assembly to the Secretary-General to continue the operation of the Transparency Registry, through the secretariat of the Commission and funded entirely by voluntary contributions until the end of 2023, and to keep the General Assembly informed of developments.[99]

288. The Commission recalled that the Transparency Registry had constituted a central feature of the Rules on Transparency by providing a consolidated, transparent and easily accessible global case record database for all investor-State arbitrations conducted under the Rules on Transparency.[100]

289. The Commission took note of the awareness-raising activities conducted by the secretariat and the tendency towards more transparency in investor-State dispute settlement. The Commission also noted that the Transparency Registry was routinely updated with new cases and the United Nations Convention on Transparency in Treaty-based Investor-State Arbitration and the Rules on Transparency were promoted by a legal officer in the UNCITRAL secretariat responsible for managing and operating the Transparency Registry. The Commission also recalled a note by the Secretariat before the Commission at its present session, which provided an update on the Rules on Transparency and the Transparency Registry (A/CN.9/1136, paras. 16 and 17) (see paras. 253 and 259 above).

290. With respect to the current budgetary situation of the Transparency Registry, the Commission noted that the Transparency Registry would continue to operate through February 2024, funded entirely by voluntary contributions from the European Union and BMZ. The Commission expressed its appreciation to the European Union and BMZ for having provided funding that allowed the secretariat to continue the project through February 2024. The Commission was informed that the secretariat was

[96] A/73/17, annex I.
[97] See the Rules on Transparency, art. 8.
[98] A/CN.9/1015, paras. 1–8; A/CN.9/1097, para. 17.
[99] General Assembly resolution 75/133, paras. 4 and 5.
[100] General Assembly resolution 70/115, para. 2.

currently in contact with interested States and intergovernmental organizations regarding funding of the project beyond February 2024.

291. With regard to the above-noted funding situation, the Commission reiterated its appeal to all States, international organizations and other interested entities to consider making contributions towards the operation of the Transparency Registry, and to make them, if possible, in the form of a multi-year contributions, so as to facilitate planning.

292. The Commission considered the future operation of the Transparency Registry. During consideration of the issue, the European Commission expressed its satisfaction with the work done by the UNCITRAL secretariat with respect to the Transparency Registry, which had resulted in improved access to information about investor-State arbitration cases conducted under the Rules on Transparency, as well as the efforts made to promote the UNCITRAL transparency standards through events organized around the world. It also expressed its belief that the Transparency Registry played a key role in the global tendency towards greater transparency in investor-State dispute resolution. The European Commission indicated that it was in the process of contributing additional funds to cover the current project until the end of June 2024 and was also planning to make an effort to continue financing the project beyond June 2024, possibly for two to three years. The Commission expressed its appreciation to the European Commission for its continued support of the project.

293. After discussion, the Commission expressed its support for the continued operation of the Transparency Registry as a key mechanism for promoting transparency in investor-State arbitration. Accordingly, the Commission recommended to the General Assembly that it request the Secretary-General to continue to operate, through the secretariat of the Commission, the Transparency Registry in accordance with article 8 of the Rules on Transparency, as a continuation of the project until the end of 2024, subject to funding. The Commission also recommended to the General Assembly that the UNCITRAL secretariat keep the General Assembly informed of developments regarding the funding and budgetary situation of the Transparency Registry based on its operation, as had been the practice.

C. Bibliography of recent writings related to the work of UNCITRAL

294. The Commission recalled that the UNCITRAL Law Library specialized in international commercial law. Its collection featured important titles and online resources in that field in the six United Nations official languages. During the reporting period, UNCITRAL Law Library had responded to approximately 445 reference requests, originating in 52 countries. Since the COVID-19 pandemic measures had been lifted, the number of visitors to the UNCITRAL Law Library had continued to increase. The Library had received 83 visitors other than meeting participants, staff and interns, including researchers from 19 countries.

295. Considering the broader impact of UNCITRAL texts, the Commission took note of the bibliography of recent writings related to the work of UNCITRAL (A/CN.9/1135) and the influence of UNCITRAL texts as described in academic and professional literature. The Commission noted, in particular that the consolidated bibliography contained more than 12,109 entries, reproduced in English and in the original language. The Commission further noted the importance of facilitating a comprehensive approach to the creation of the bibliography and the need to remain informed of activities of organizations active in the field of international trade law. In that regard, the Commission recalled and repeated its request that organizations invited to the Commission's annual sessions donate copies of their journals, reports and other publications to the UNCITRAL Law Library.[101] The Commission expressed appreciation to all organizations that donated materials.

---

[101] *Official Records of the General Assembly, Seventieth Session, Supplement No. 17* (A/70/17), para. 264.

XVII. Current role of UNCITRAL in promoting the rule of law

A. Introduction

296. The Commission recalled that the item on the current role of UNCITRAL in promoting the rule of law had been on the agenda of the Commission since its forty-first session, in 2008,[102] in response to the General Assembly's invitation to the Commission to comment, in its report to the General Assembly, on the Commission's current role in promoting the rule of law.[103] The Commission further recalled that, at its forty-first to fifty-fifth sessions, in 2008 to 2022, respectively, the Commission, in its annual reports to the General Assembly,[104] had transmitted comments on its role in promoting the rule of law at the national and international levels.

297. At the present session, the Commission had before it a note by the Secretariat on the role of UNCITRAL in promoting the rule of law at the national and international levels (A/CN.9/1147). The Commission noted that the General Assembly, in resolution 77/110, had reiterated its invitation to the Commission to comment on its current role in promoting the rule of law. The Commission noted that the same resolution had indicated that the upcoming debates of the Sixth Committee under the agenda item on the rule of law would focus on the subtopic, "Using technology to advance access to justice for all".[105] (For comments of the Commission transmitted to the General Assembly under this agenda item, as requested in para. 20 of General Assembly resolution 77/110, see sect. B below.)

298. The Commission highlighted the relevance of its work to the promotion of the rule of law and the implementation of the Sustainable Development Goals. The Commission reiterated its request to States, the secretariat, organizations and institutions to continue their efforts to increase awareness of the role of UNCITRAL standards and activities for the promotion of the rule of law at the national and international levels and of their contribution to the implementation of the Sustainable Development Goals. In that context, the Commission noted that the high-level political forum on sustainable development, which usually took place in parallel with annual sessions of UNCITRAL, provided an annual opportunity for States, the secretariat, organizations and institutions to highlight the role of UNCITRAL in the implementation of the Sustainable Development Goals.[106] The Commission also noted that another opportunity was provided by consultations, led by Rwanda and Sweden, leading to the Summit of the Future in September 2024, at which a global digital compact was expected to be agreed outlining "shared principles for an open, free and secure digital future for all". The Commission further noted that discussions so far between the secretariat and the Office of the Envoy of the Secretary-General on

---

[102] For the decision of the Commission to include the item on its agenda, see *Official Records of the General Assembly, Sixty-second Session, Supplement No. 17* (A/62/17), part two, paras. 111–113.

[103] General Assembly resolutions 62/70, para. 3; 63/128, para. 7; 64/116, para. 9; 65/32, para. 10; 66/102, para. 12; 67/97, para. 14; 68/116, para. 14; 69/123, para. 17; 70/118, para. 20; 71/148, para. 22; 72/119, para. 25; 73/207, para. 20; 74/191, para. 20; 75/141, para. 20; 76/117, para. 20; and 77/110, para. 20.

[104] *Official Records of the General Assembly, Sixty-third Session, Supplement No. 17* and corrigendum (A/63/17 and A/63/17/Corr.1), para. 386; ibid., *Sixty-fourth Session, Supplement No. 17* (A/64/17), paras. 413–419; ibid., *Sixty-fifth Session, Supplement No. 17* (A/65/17), paras. 313–336; ibid., *Sixty-sixth Session, Supplement No. 17* (A/66/17), paras. 299–321; ibid., *Sixty-seventh Session, Supplement No. 17* (A/67/17), paras. 195–227; ibid., *Sixty-eighth Session, Supplement No. 17* (A/68/17), paras. 267–291; ibid., *Sixty-ninth Session, Supplement No. 17* (A/69/17), paras. 215–240; A/70/17, paras. 318–324; A/71/17, paras. 317–342; A/72/17, paras. 435–441; A/73/17, paras. 232–233; A/74/17, paras. 303–308; A/75/17, para. 25; A/76/17, paras. 370–374; and A/77/17, paras. 308–315.

[105] General Assembly resolution 77/110, para. 23.

[106] For example, the theme of the Forum held from 10 to19 July 2023 was "Accelerating the recovery from the coronavirus (COVID-19) and the full implementation of the 2030 Agenda for Sustainable Development at all levels", with a focus on Sustainable Development Goal 6 on clean water and sanitation, Goal 9 on industry, innovation and infrastructure, Goal 11 on sustainable cities and communities, and Goal 17 on partnerships for the Goals.

Technology indicated that UNCITRAL texts and principles on electronic commerce could be used, with the support of the recently finalized legal taxonomy,[107] as a foundation for developing the legal infrastructure to support the global digital compact.

B. UNCITRAL comments to the General Assembly

299. In formulating its comments to the General Assembly in response to the invitation contained in paragraph 23 of General Assembly resolution 77/110, the Commission bore in mind the subtopic of the upcoming debates of the Sixth Committee on the rule of law: "Using technology to advance access to justice for all". The comments reviewed discussion of the subtopic at prior sessions and described relevant exploratory work.

300. The Commission recalled its consideration of issues relevant to that subtopic at its sessions in 2014,[108] 2016,[109] 2017[110] and 2022.[111] At its forty-seventh session, in 2014, in the comments by the Commission on its role in promoting the rule of law and facilitating access to justice, the Commission had noted that technology tools such as the UNCITRAL website, CLOUT, digests and the Transparency Registry, as well as training tools, were relevant for increasing legal awareness and legal empowerment and provided a foundation for the promotion of uniform interpretation and the application of international commercial law standards, thus increasing access to justice.[112] At its forty-ninth session, in 2016, in a summary of a panel discussion on practical measures to facilitate access to justice in the commercial law context, in particular by MSMEs, technological solutions to access to justice issues had been noted.[113] At its fiftieth session in 2017, in a summary of the UNCITRAL Congress 2017, the Commission had heard about a panel on new frontiers in dispute resolution and technological solutions that would enhance access to justice. At its fifty-fifth session in 2022, in noting the links between the work programme of the Commission and the Sustainable Development Goals and the rule of law, the Commission had highlighted the project on the stocktaking of developments in dispute resolution in the digital economy and noted that the project could provide the international community with concrete information on how technology could be utilized to improve dispute resolution and access to justice with the aim of ensuring that use of technology would further enable access to justice while maintaining fairness and due process.

301. At the present session, the Commission highlighted how the ongoing project on stocktaking of dispute resolution in the digital economy contributed to the advancement of access to justice through technology and how its outcome, which was expected to contain proposals on possible future legislative work in the area of dispute resolution, might further increase access to justice. The Commission noted that the UNCITRAL secretariat was currently compiling, analysing and sharing relevant information on the changing landscape of dispute resolution with increased digitalization and that both the positive and negative impacts of the use of technology in dispute resolution were being considered in the stocktaking project.

302. On the positive side, it was said that there had been a significant increase in the use of technology in alternative dispute resolution and such use had been accelerated by the COVID-19 pandemic. That development had led to a broader acceptance of the integration of technologies into dispute resolution services, which in turn had expanded access to such services. Courts had also embraced technology to increase

---

[107] A/77/17, para. 165.
[108] A/69/17, paras. 234–240.
[109] A/71/17, paras. 332–342.
[110] A/72/17, para. 408.
[111] A/77/17, para. 314.
[112] A/69/17, para. 240 (b).
[113] A/71/17, paras. 337 and 338.

the efficiency of the dispute resolution process, making it less costly, less time-consuming and more accessible. Use of technology could also be climate friendly and cost-effective because it could reduce the need to travel. There were also potential negative impacts of the use of technology in dispute resolution. The integrity of the dispute resolution process needed to be maintained when using or incorporating new technology, especially the principles of due process and fairness. For example, differing levels of access to technology and technology infrastructure across and even within jurisdictions could affect due process and fairness. Similarly, the provision of platform-based dispute resolution services might need further scrutiny.

303. The Commission also highlighted the continued expansion of the e-learning modules on the work of UNCITRAL (see para. 250 above). It was explained that the e-learning modules provided a general introduction to the work of UNCITRAL, outlined how UNCITRAL texts would contribute to the achievement of the Sustainable Development Goals, and included subject-specific overviews of certain UNCITRAL texts.

304. The Commission noted the expected contribution of its ongoing work on investor-State dispute settlement reform, civil asset tracing in insolvency proceedings, applicable law in insolvency proceedings, and negotiable cargo documents to the achievement of the Sustainable Development Goals.

XVIII. Relevant General Assembly resolutions

A. Resolutions adopted by the General Assembly at its seventy-seventh session

305. The Commission recalled that, at its fiftieth session, in 2017, it had requested the secretariat to replace an oral report to the Commission on relevant General Assembly resolutions with a written report to be issued before the session.[114] Pursuant to that request, the Commission had before it, at its current session, a note by the Secretariat (A/CN.9/1141) summarizing the content of the operative paragraphs of General Assembly resolution 77/99 on the report of UNCITRAL on the work of its fifty-fifth session, resolution 77/100 on the United Nations Convention on the International Effects of Judicial Sales of Ships, and resolution 77/101 on the UNCITRAL Model Law on the Use and Cross-border Recognition of Identity Management and Trust Services.

306. The Commission took note of those General Assembly resolutions.

B. Streamlining and simplifying future resolutions on the work of UNCITRAL

307. The Commission noted that the length of the resolutions adopted by the General Assembly after consideration of the report of UNCITRAL on the work of its annual sessions (also known as "UNCITRAL omnibus resolutions") had increased over time. The Commission heard expressions of concern about the readability of the UNCITRAL omnibus resolutions in the future if that trend were to continue because the continuous increase in the length of resolutions and the number of operative paragraphs was likely to distract the reader from the focus on the Commission's mandate and the work accomplished at its annual sessions. In addition, other matters of immediate interest and which deserved greater attention would appear diluted in the reiteration of language carried over from previous resolutions.

308. The Commission heard a proposal for streamlining the UNCITRAL omnibus resolutions, which included the following guiding principles: (a) limiting references to past events and decisions to three years prior to the date of the resolution to be

[114] A/72/17, para. 480.

adopted; (b) reorganizing the UNCITRAL omnibus resolution so that there would be only one or two operative paragraphs addressing each thematic topic of the work of UNCITRAL; (c) shortening the length of paragraphs and consolidating them where appropriate; (d) giving preference to action-oriented language in operative paragraphs; (e) deleting preambular paragraphs and operative paragraphs which did not contain necessary basic information or recent updates on developments in the work of UNCITRAL; and (f) limiting references to specific subjects (e.g. the rule of law) to one or two paragraphs.

309. While broad support was expressed for streamlining future UNCITRAL omnibus resolutions, many delegations noted that more time would be needed for them to consult internally on the proposed guiding principles, especially concerning the proposed three-year limit for references to past events or decisions. It was noted that adoption of resolutions on the work of UNCITRAL by the Sixth Committee of the General Assembly had generally been relatively easy and less political compared with the adoption of General Assembly resolutions on other subjects. It was added that any attempt to deviate from text that had appeared in previous resolutions might make them more prone to further amendments. A query was raised as to the connection between the work of the Commission and the content of the UNCITRAL omnibus resolutions. It was explained that UNCITRAL omnibus resolutions were prepared on the basis of the annual reports of the Commission.

310. After discussion, the Commission requested the secretariat to facilitate an open and flexible intersessional consultative process among Member States with a view to developing guidelines on streamlining and simplifying the text of future UNCITRAL omnibus resolutions, and to report back thereon to the Commission at its next session, in 2024.

XIX. Other business

A. Evaluation of the role of the UNCITRAL secretariat in facilitating the work of the Commission

311. An online questionnaire on the level of satisfaction of UNCITRAL with the services provided by its secretariat had been sent to States. The Commission was informed that 56 responses had been received and that the level of satisfaction with the services provided by the secretariat remained high. On average, respondents gave a rating of 4.75 out of 5 for "the services and support provided to the Commission", and respondents gave a rating of 4.63 out of 5 for "the availability of information on the UNCITRAL website".

312. The Commission expressed appreciation to its secretariat for its work.

B. Side events

313. The Commission welcomed the initiative of the secretariat and several States in organizing side events to its fifty-sixth session. During the first week, four side events relating to the work of investor-State dispute settlement reform took place addressing the following: (a) the quantum of damages in investor-State dispute settlement, and the perspective of developing countries; (b) implementing the code of conduct for arbitrators in international investment dispute resolution; (c) revision of the IBA Guidelines on Conflicts of Interest; and (d) dispute prevention in investor-State dispute settlement. During the second week, one side event was organized by Paraguay to present the Chaco Vivo project to illustrate forest preservation and carbon sequestration. During the last week, three additional side events took place focusing on (a) new frontiers of digital trade, (b) empowering women in international trade and (c) the signing ceremony of the United Nations Convention on the International Effects of Judicial Sales of Ships.

XX. Date and place of future meetings

A. Fifty-seventh session of the Commission

314. The Commission approved the holding of its fifty-seventh session in New York, from 24 June to 12 July 2024. (It was noted that the United Nations Headquarters would be closed on 4 July 2024). Depending on the expected workload of the session, the secretariat was requested to optimize the duration of the session to the extent possible.

B. Sessions of working groups

315. The Commission considered conference service requirements in light of its work programme, reports of its working groups and a note by the Secretariat (A/CN.9/1121). It approved the following schedule of working group sessions in the second half of 2023 and in 2024, taking note that the dates proposed below included the following significant holidays of the United Nations: 25 September 2023 – Yom Kippur (which would fall on the first day of the tentative dates of the fortieth session of Working Group I); and 27 November 2023 – Gurpurab (which would fall on the first day of the tentative dates of the forty-third session of Working Group VI). The Secretariat was encouraged to find alternative weeks for working group sessions in the second half of 2024 so as to avoid back-to-back meetings and to take into account other scheduling concerns noted in the discussion.

	Second half of 2023 (Vienna)	*First half of 2024 (New York unless noted otherwise)*	*Second half of 2024 (Vienna) (to be confirmed by the Commission at its fifty-seventh session, in 2024)*
Working Group I (Warehouse Receipts)	40th session 25–29 September 2023 *(25 September 2023 falls on Yom Kippur)*	41st session 5–9 February 2024	42nd session *2–6 September 2024*
Working Group II (Dispute Settlement)	78th session 18–22 September 2023	79th session 12–16 February 2024	80th session *30 September–4 October 2024*
Working Group III (Investor-State Dispute Settlement Reform)	46th session 9–13 October 2023	47th session (*Vienna*) 22–26 January 2024 48th session 1–5 April 2024	49th session *23–27 September 2024*
Working Group IV (Electronic Commerce)	66th session 16–20 October 2023	67th session 15–19 April 2024	68th session *18–22 November 2024*
Working Group V (Insolvency Law)	63rd session 11–15 December 2023	64th session 13–17 May 2024	65th session *25–29 November 2024*
Working Group VI (Negotiable Cargo Documents)	43rd session 27 November–1 December 2023 *(27 November 2023 falls on Gurpurab)*	44th session 6–10 May 2024	45th session *9–13 December 2024*

Annex I

UNCITRAL Model Provisions on Mediation for International Investment Disputes

Provision 1
Availability and commencement of mediation

1. "Mediation" means a process, irrespective of the expression used or the basis upon which the process is carried out, whereby parties attempt to reach an amicable settlement of their dispute with the assistance of a third person or persons (the "mediator") lacking the authority to impose a solution upon the parties to the dispute.

2. The parties should consider mediation to settle an international investment dispute amicably.

3. The parties may agree to engage in mediation at any time, including after the commencement of any other dispute resolution proceeding.

4. A party may invite the other party in writing to engage in mediation in accordance with provision 2 (the "invitation").

5. The other party should make all reasonable efforts to accept or reject the invitation in writing within 30 days of receipt of the invitation. If the inviting party does not receive an acceptance within 60 days of receipt of the invitation, that party may elect to treat it as a rejection of the invitation.

6. The parties shall agree to conduct the mediation in accordance with these Provisions and:

(a) The United Nations Commission on International Trade Law (UNCITRAL) Mediation Rules;

(b) The International Centre for Settlement of Investment Disputes (ICSID) Mediation Rules;

(c) The International Bar Association (IBA) Rules for Investor-State Mediation; or

(d) Any other rules.

7. Unless provided otherwise in the rules agreed by the parties pursuant to paragraph 6:

(a) The mediation shall be deemed to have commenced on the day on which the other party accepts the invitation;

(b) The parties shall appoint a mediator within 30 days of the commencement of the mediation. If a mediator is not appointed within that period of time, the parties shall agree on an institution or a person that shall assist them in appointing a mediator; and

(c) The mediator shall convene a meeting with the parties within 15 days after the appointment, and the parties shall attend that meeting.

8. The parties may at any time agree to exclude or vary any of these Provisions.

9. Where any of these Provisions is in conflict with a provision of the law applicable to the mediation from which the parties cannot derogate, including any applicable instrument or court order, that provision of the law shall prevail.

Provision 2
Information required in an invitation

The invitation to engage in mediation referred to in provision 1, paragraph 4, shall contain at least the following information:

(a) The name and contact details of the inviting party and its legal representative and, if the invitation is made by a legal person, the place of its incorporation;

(b) Government agencies and entities that have been involved in the matters giving rise to the invitation;

(c) A description of the basis of the dispute sufficient to identify the matters giving rise to the invitation; and

(d) A description of any prior steps taken to resolve the dispute, including information on any pending claim.

Provision 3
Relationship with arbitration and other proceedings to resolve the dispute

1. Upon the commencement of the mediation, a party shall not initiate or continue any other proceeding to resolve the dispute until the mediation is terminated.

2. If the mediation commences while another proceeding to resolve the dispute is in progress, the parties shall request the suspension of that proceeding pursuant to the rules applicable to that proceeding.

Provision 4
Use of information in other proceedings

A party shall not rely in other proceedings on any positions taken, admissions or offers of settlement made or views expressed by the other party or the mediator during the mediation.

Provision 5
Settlement agreement

The parties should consider whether the settlement agreement resulting from mediation meets the requirements set forth in the United Nations Convention on International Settlement Agreements Resulting from Mediation.

Annex II

UNCITRAL Guidelines on Mediation for International Investment Disputes

A. Purpose

1. The purpose of the UNCITRAL Guidelines on Mediation for International Investment Disputes (the "Guidelines") is to explain how mediation can be utilized to resolve international investment disputes. The Guidelines do not intend to promote best practice, but rather list and describe briefly issues that should be considered when undertaking mediation for international investment disputes. Owing to the flexible nature of mediation, the procedural styles, practices, and methods that lead parties to a settlement of a dispute may vary. The Guidelines assist parties in understanding the different aspects of mediation for international investment disputes, the nuances of the process and the possible benefits. The parties and the mediator may use or refer to the Guidelines at their discretion and to the extent they see fit, and need not adopt or provide reasons for not adopting any particular element of the Guidelines. The Guidelines do not impose any legal requirements binding upon the parties or the mediator and are not suitable to be used as mediation rules.

B. Availability of mediation to resolve international investment disputes

2. Mediation is a flexible process whereby a third person (the "mediator") assists the parties to negotiate an amicable settlement of the issues in dispute. It is an effective tool to resolve disputes with the mediator structuring and facilitating a dialogue between the parties. Mediation allows the parties to exercise control over the process, to reach a self-tailored outcome and to preserve their relationship. Additionally, the involvement of a mediator provides necessary safeguards for due process, which is important as the outcome of the negotiations may be scrutinized or challenged by the public. As a form of assisted or facilitated negotiation, mediation can be useful when negotiations between the parties are considered most suitable for resolving a dispute. Therefore, mediation can also be an effective tool to resolve international investment disputes.

C. Suitability of mediation to resolve an international investment dispute

3. In considering whether mediation is suitable to settle any issue or dispute arising out of an international investment, the following are some of the aspects, if relevant, to be taken into account:

(a) Desirability of maintaining the parties' relationship also in light of retaining the current investments as well as the possibility of attracting future investments;

(b) Willingness of the parties to enter into a dialogue or negotiations and understand the other party's positions;

(c) Number of the parties involved, including those with potentially different interests;

(d) Desirability of resolving a dispute in a time- and cost-effective manner;

(e) Nature of the dispute and the underlying grievance;

(f) Complexity of the issues in dispute and urgency to address them;

(g) Usefulness for the parties to streamline the issues at stake;

(h) Desirability of involving a third party;

(i) Desirability of the parties having control over the resolution process and the outcome;

(j) Desirability of the parties developing tailored and creative solutions;

(k) Any implication of complying with any settlement agreement, including any political, economic, social and financial implication.

4. While the above checklist can assist the parties in determining the suitability of mediation for resolving an issue or a dispute, not all aspects may be relevant. The suitability of mediation might differ depending on the perspective of each party. While some parties may find mediation suitable early on, for example, prior to an issue being escalated into a dispute, others may find it suitable after the initiation of arbitration or litigation or at a later stage of such proceedings (for example, after the written statements or a hearing).

D. Consent to mediate

5. Mediation is a consensual process that is based on the parties' agreement to that process. States may express their consent to mediation in investment treaties, investment contracts, domestic legislation or in any other form. Consent to mediation can also be expressed as part of a multi-tier dispute resolution clause, which provides, for example, that when a dispute arises, parties are bound to perform certain steps, for instance, to attempt mediation before commencing arbitration.

6. Consent to mediation does not need to be expressed prior to the dispute. A party wishing to mediate can invite the other party to mediation, which may include a description of the basis of the dispute sufficient to identify the matters giving rise to the dispute, and a description of any prior steps taken to resolve the dispute, including any information on pending claims.

7. There may be instances where parties are required to take part in mediation prior to initiating arbitration or litigation. However, as a consensual process, parties are generally free to leave the process at any time. Some mediation rules[1] and treaties provide that once mediation is initiated, it should continue for a certain period of time or until a certain stage of the process.

E. Timing and duration of mediation

8. While the suitability of mediation may change with the evolving circumstances, it is available at any point in time. It can thus be employed as a tool throughout the life cycle of an investment whenever issues or disputes arise. Investment treaties and contracts may specify a period of time, during which parties are encouraged to reach an amicable settlement including possibly through mediation. In certain instances, the lapse of that period may be a precondition for initiating arbitration.

9. Mediation may resolve some of the underlying issues, which might help de-escalating the dispute or narrowing it down. In general, it is easier to find solutions mutually agreeable to the parties if mediation takes place prior to the parties taking adversarial positions.

10. When parties agree to mediate, they may wish to set a time period during which they will engage in mediation. The duration should not be too short and be sufficient to conduct mediation in an efficient and streamlined manner.

[1] For example, art. 9, para. 4, of the Rules for Investor-State Mediation of the International Bar Association requires parties to participate in the mediation management conference.

F. Mediation rules

11. When parties express their consent or agree to mediate, they should also agree on and refer to a set of rules to govern the mediation process. The Mediation Rules of the International Centre for Settlement of Investment Disputes of 2022 (ICSID Mediation Rules)[2] and the Rules for Investor-State Mediation of the International Bar Association of 2012 (IBA Rules) are examples of rules tailored to international investment disputes. Parties may also refer to the generic UNCITRAL Mediation Rules adopted in 2021[3] or any other set of mediation rules. Mediation rules provide a procedural framework for mediation, assist the parties in avoiding procedural lacunae and at the same time provide flexibility to the parties to tailor the procedure to their needs. However, where such rules or the agreement of the parties are in conflict with provisions of law applicable to the mediation which the parties cannot derogate from, the provisions of the applicable law would prevail.[4]

G. Role of institutions

12. As a form of facilitated negotiation, mediation can be conducted with or without the administrative support of institutions. Administrative support offered by institutions includes, for instance: (a) guidance on procedural aspects; (b) assistance in communicating with the other party, including conveying an offer to mediate; (c) identification of a pool of mediators and assistance in their selection and appointment; (d) assistance in the logistical aspects of mediation, including the organization of in-person and remote meetings as well as providing for data protection and cybersecurity measures; (e) financial services (for example, requesting, holding and managing advance payments by the parties to cover the costs of the mediation and processing of mediator fees and expenses); and (f) issuance of a certification that mediation took place.[5]

13. Such institutions may also raise awareness about the availability of mediation, provide general information – including on best practices – and conduct capacity-building activities for interested parties and potential mediators.

H. Role, qualification and appointment of a mediator

1. Role of a mediator

14. A mediator facilitates the parties' negotiations and assists the parties in arriving at a mutually agreeable solution. Accordingly, a mediator does not decide how the dispute shall be resolved but rather supports the parties in resolving the issues themselves through negotiation. A mediator creates a neutral environment for the parties to discuss, overcome deadlocks and arrive at a solution.

15. A mediator should not take decisions, make judgments over the parties' past conduct that led to the dispute nor offer legal advice to the parties. A mediator may, however, assist the parties in assessing the strengths and weaknesses of their arguments.

---

[2] Available at https://icsid.worldbank.org/rules-regulations/mediation.

[3] Available at https://uncitral.un.org/en/texts/mediation.

[4] See the UNCITRAL Mediation Rules, art. 1, para. 5; ICSID Mediation Rules, rule 3, para. 3; IBA Rules, art. 1, para. 3.

[5] Such a certificate may assist parties in enforcing a settlement agreement under the United Nations Convention on International Settlement Agreements Resulting from Mediation or meeting other requirements in investment treaties (for example, as proof that mediation took place when initiating arbitration).

2. Qualifications and other requirements of a mediator

16. Given the above-mentioned role, a mediator should be an experienced professional with recognized competence in carrying out mediation. A mediator should be experienced in various means of communication and different negotiation styles and be capable of utilizing tools to assist the parties as they develop mutually acceptable solutions. A mediator should be able to take into account the needs, interests, concerns, constraints, and motivations of all the parties.

17. *Competency.* When choosing a mediator, parties should consider whether the mediator possesses, among others, the following experiences and competencies (see also para. 22 below):[6]

(a) Experience as a mediator;

(b) Ability to conduct mediation in an effective manner;

(c) Mediation training, including any accreditation;

(d) Experience working in or with Governments or State entities;

(e) Experience in different forms of dispute resolution involving Governments or State entities;

(f) Expertise in the field of investment law or in the relevant sector (see para. 18 below);

(g) Understanding of the context and framework of investment disputes, including economic, legal, social and cultural aspects;

(h) Knowledge of one or more languages to communicate effectively with the parties and understand the issues at hand.

18. While expertise and knowledge of investment law could be beneficial in probing the strengths and weaknesses of the parties' positions, such legal expertise might not be the key competency considering that the main task of a mediator lies with facilitating the negotiations between the parties. Should legal expertise be required in mediation, a legal expert could be appointed to assist the mediator and the parties' legal representatives could provide their clients with the legal evaluation of the dispute or any given proposed solution (see para. 27 below).

19. *Independence and Impartiality.* A mediator should be independent and impartial.[7] A mediator should therefore disclose relevant information to enable the parties to become aware of any conflicts of interest.[8]

20. *Nationality.* The nationality of the mediator may also be a factor to be taken into account when selecting a mediator. For example, parties may consider whether the appointment of a mediator of a nationality other than those of the parties would avoid any perception of bias. However, the parties may also consider whether there might be benefits in selecting a mediator with the same nationality, for example, such a mediator would be familiar with their language, customs and culture and the acceptability of the resulting settlement agreement might be enhanced.

3. Appointment of a mediator

21. A mediator is typically appointed by the parties.[9] Parties may agree on the mediator or the appointment procedure, which may involve an institution or another

---

[6] For a list of competencies, see, for example, appendix B to the IBA Rules; the Energy Charter Secretariat, "Guide on investment mediation", 2016; and the International Mediation Institute, "Competency criteria for investor-State mediators", 2016.

[7] See the ICSID Mediation Rules, rule 12, para. 1, and the IBA Rules, art. 3.

[8] See the UNCITRAL Mediation Rules, art. 3, para. 6; the ICSID Mediation Rules, rule 14, para. 3 (b); and the IBA Rules, art. 3, paras. 3 and 4.

[9] See the UNCITRAL Mediation Rules, art. 3, para 2; the ICSID Mediation Rules, rule 13, para 1; and the IBA Rules, art. 4, para. 5.

person.[10] Under certain mediation rules, if the parties have not appointed or cannot agree on a mediator within a certain time frame, they may request an institution or another person to make the appointment (see para. 12 above).[11] Such institution should take into account geographical diversity and gender when appointing a mediator.

Number of mediators and co-mediation

22. Parties are free to agree on the number of mediators and may wish to consider appointing two mediators (referred to as "co-mediation"). Both co-mediators may be appointed jointly by the parties. Co-mediation requires mediators to possess team-working skills to jointly facilitate the parties' negotiations. As mediators may have different backgrounds or areas of expertise, co-mediation may be beneficial in complex disputes and in cases where a multitude of parties is involved or cultural diversity needs to be bridged.

23. When considering prospective mediators, particularly co-mediators, parties should strive to take into account geographical diversity and gender,[12] which could facilitate the parties' negotiations and increase the confidence in mediation.

4. Resignation and replacement of a mediator

24. There may be instances where a mediator wishes to, or needs to, resign from the mediation, at which point the mediator should inform the parties as soon as possible. In addition, if requested jointly by the parties or if the mediator is not in a position to perform the duties required, the mediator should resign from the process. Upon the resignation of a mediator, the parties would usually replace the mediator using the same procedure used to make the original appointment.

I. Role of the parties and other participants in mediation

25. Mediation requires the active participation of the parties, without which the proceedings cannot advance. The parties need to work together and with the mediator to explore the issues in dispute and generate potential solutions. The discussions may be conducted jointly with all parties or in separate meetings between the mediator and one of the parties. Facilitating negotiations by way of separate meetings is a common feature of mediation and allows the mediator to explore freely with the respective parties their interests and concerns and to develop possible options for settlement.

26. *Composition of the parties' teams.* In determining the size and composition of their team, parties should consider including a member vested with the authority to settle the dispute and to have that member present throughout the process. However, this might not be possible if, for instance, the approval or sign-off by a ministry, ministries or a cabinet is required on the side of the State, or the same by a board of directors or corporate oversight body on the side of the investor. In any case, it is desirable to include a member having a clear line of communication with the person or entity with settlement authority. Information about the authority of the participants in the mediation to settle should be shared with the mediator and the other parties at an early stage of the mediation.

27. *Role of the legal representatives.* The role of legal representatives in mediation, if any, differs from that in adversarial processes. For example, in arbitration, legal representatives usually focus on making legal and factual arguments with the goal of persuading the arbitral tribunal in issuing an award in favour of their clients. In

[10] See the UNCITRAL Mediation Rules, art. 3, para. 3; the ICSID Mediation Rules, rule 13, para. 3; and the IBA Rules, art. 4, para. 6.

[11] For example, the Secretary General of ICSID in accordance with the ICSID Mediation Rules, rule 13, para. 4, and the Secretary-General of the Permanent Court of Arbitration in accordance with the IBA Rules, art. 4, para. 7.

[12] See the UNCITRAL Mediation Rules, art. 3, para. 5.

mediation, legal representatives would take a collaborative approach in exploring and identifying future-oriented solutions that further the interest and goals of their clients. In this sense, legal representatives guide the parties through the mediation process. Legal representatives may also provide legal advice (for example, informing the parties about the possibility of mediation and available mediation rules), assist with a realistic assessment of the strengths and weaknesses of the case, assist the parties in drafting written statements, and identify and compile relevant documents to be used in mediation. Legal representatives may also be involved in the discussions on procedural matters, the preparation of opening statements, and drafting the terms of a potential settlement agreement.

Experts and other parties

28. The parties may wish to consider whether the participation of experts and other parties in the mediation might be beneficial and assist the parties in achieving an amicable solution.

29. *Role of experts.* A party's team may include subject-matter experts, who would advise the party, for example, on financial matters relevant for generating offers or the terms of a settlement agreement. The parties may also consider jointly appointing an expert, whose input may be beneficial in negotiating a mutually agreeable solution. The type of participation and the scope of the expert's input would be determined by the parties in consultation with the mediator.

30. *Role of other parties.* The flexibility of mediation allows for the participation of other parties in the process. The parties should consider whether the participation of third parties (including through written statements) could be one way to take into account the public interest in international investment disputes and might assist in achieving an amicable solution. Examples of such parties include: (a) States parties to the underlying investment treaty not party to the dispute; (b) local communities affected by the investment, the dispute, or any negotiated solution; (c) the civil society at large; and (d) other interested stakeholders. The scope and the procedural framework for their participation would need to be determined by the parties in consultation with the mediator.

J. Conduct of mediation for international investment disputes

Different phases

31. Mediation may consist of different phases depending on the issues at hand.[13] The following is an illustrative example of the different phases.

[13] See ICSID, "Background paper on investment mediation", July 2021, p. 12.

Phases				
Preparation/initial consultation	*Facilitated dialogue*			*Conclusion settlement/termination*
	Opening	*Exploration*	*Developing options*	
Parties provide the mediator with initial written statements with a short description of the issues and their views on those issues. The mediator discusses the procedural aspects with the parties. In this phase, the procedure to be followed, the mediator's approach and style are discussed.	Each party (or their representative) provides an opening statement.	The mediator engages with the parties to identify the foundation of or outline a mutually acceptable solution.	The mediator assists the parties in developing options for settlement.	The parties record the terms of their settlement agreement and ensure that the agreement complies with the requirements of the applicable law. If the mediation does not result in a settlement, it should be terminated, which should be recorded in clear terms as it may form the basis for any subsequent procedures or impact limitation periods.

In-person and online mediation

32. Meetings held during mediation may be held in person or remotely using online means. While mediation has traditionally been conducted in person, technology has allowed for a significant increase in the number of online mediations in recent years. In-person meetings allow for direct interaction between the parties and the mediator and could be beneficial to the mediator and the parties to build rapport, which facilitates the negotiations. Remote online meetings do not require travel and may address scheduling conflicts, leading to a more time- and cost-effective process. As long as the parties are able to easily access the meetings, online meetings could be useful for conducting parts of or the entirety of the mediation process.

33. Online mediation may, however, pose challenges regarding data protection and cybersecurity, which might affect the integrity of the process. Accordingly, applicable privacy policies and whether the data processing and retention policies of online platforms provide sufficient robust protection should be considered. Measures should be put in place to ensure a level of security for those engaging on online platforms. Additional safeguards may be implemented to ensure the integrity of the process such as: (a) measures to ensure privacy of the proceedings (for example, data minimalization, encryption, and digital attestation); and (b) a contractual stipulation that prohibits the other parties from publicizing or utilizing confidential information in subsequent adversarial hearings. Such considerations may be stipulated in confidentiality arrangements addressing, for example, the use of password-protected conferences and/or prohibition of audio and video recordings of the negotiations.

34. In any case, the advantages and disadvantages of conducting mediation in person and online should be discussed between the parties and the mediator at the outset of the mediation.

K. Treatment of information exchanged: Use of information in other proceedings, confidentiality, and disclosure obligations

Use of information in other proceedings

35. For mediation to be successful, the parties must be able to freely engage in the negotiations without being concerned that the information exchanged, or statements made during that process will be used by the other party in another proceeding, for example, as evidence. For this purpose, parties typically agree to not use information exchanged during the mediation in other proceedings, which applies to all those

involved in the mediation process.[14] This encourages discussions by preventing statements made or information exchanged in a genuine attempt to settle a dispute from being relied upon by the other party in any other proceeding. However, if the information or document is available independent of the mediation, such information does not become inadmissible merely as a consequence of having been exchanged in mediation.[15]

Confidentiality and transparency

36. Parties should consider whether the confidentiality of the mediation proceedings as well as information and documents shared therein is necessary to enable an open and frank discussion. If so, the confidentiality obligation should begin with the commencement of mediation and apply to all those involved in the mediation. Parties should be assured that they can share confidential information and engage in substantive discussions without fearing any negative consequences. Therefore, confidentiality may be an important advantage of mediation.

37. On the other hand, parties should also consider whether transparency may be relevant in light of the public interest and the possible expenditure of public funds with regard to international investment disputes. In order to ensure public acceptance and to enhance the legitimacy of mediation for international investment disputes, a balance should be struck between confidentiality and transparency.

38. Parties wishing to specifically address confidentiality and transparency in mediation for international investment disputes should agree on those aspects. When choosing mediation rules, the parties should consider whether the provisions therein are appropriate for international investment disputes and balance confidentiality and transparency. Aspects that parties may wish to consider include: (a) whether the fact that mediation took place should be confidential; (b) whether information relating to or obtained during the mediation should be confidential; (c) whether and to what extent agreed settlements should be confidential; (d) the extent to which experts and other parties should have access to confidential information; (e) media or public disclosure protocols to provide updates to the public and/or relevant constituents during the mediation; and (f) the extent of disclosure in the event of unsuccessful mediation.

39. There may be instances where the level of confidentiality that can be agreed to by the parties is limited. For example, disclosure may be required in domestic legislation or international agreements, or by domestic courts (referred to as affirmative disclosure requirements). Further examples may be found in the domestic legislation applicable to the underlying transaction or dispute (such as domestic legislation governing public-private partnerships,[16] public financial management regulations, budget transparency legislation, or freedom of information legislation) and/or to mediation participants. There are also instances in which domestic legislation on disclosure of information aimed at safeguarding the public interest require the publication of any agreed engagement and/or ongoing disclosure of performance, as well as any negotiated terms.

---

[14] This approach is found in mediation rules (see the UNCITRAL Mediation Rules, art. 7; the ICSID Mediation Rules, rule 11) as well as in a number of recent investment agreements, for example, art. 25, para. 1, of the agreement between Argentina and Japan for the promotion and protection of investment ("Argentina–Japan BIT (2018)"), and art. 9.18, para. 3, of the Comprehensive and Progressive Agreement for Trans-Pacific Partnership (CPTPP) (2018); see also art. 8.20, para. 2, of the Comprehensive Economic and Trade Agreement between Canada and the European Union (CETA) (2016).

[15] UNCITRAL Mediation Rules, art. 7, para. 4.

[16] The World Bank's Framework for Disclosure in Public-Private Partnerships is illustrative of the objectives and scope of such disclosure regimes. See, for example, World Bank Group, Construction Sector Transparency Initiative and Public-Private Infrastructure Advisory Facility, *A Framework for Disclosure in Public-Private Partnerships: Technical Guidance for Systematic, Proactive, Pre-and Post-Procurement Disclosure of Information in Public-Private Partnership Programs*, August 2015.

L. Settlement agreement

40. In mediation, parties are in control of the process and are expected to be actively engaged in the process in good faith. This means that a settlement agreement including the terms therein is not imposed on the parties until it is agreed by them. Given the voluntary nature, parties are expected to comply with the terms of any negotiated settlement agreement. Nevertheless, to ensure validity of the settlement agreement, parties should be mindful of form and content requirements. Additionally, in the event enforcement is sought, requirements related to filing, registration and delivery may become relevant. For example, the requirements in the United Nations Convention on International Settlement Agreements Resulting from Mediation ("Singapore Convention") and the UNCITRAL Model Law on International Commercial Mediation and International Settlement Agreements Resulting from Mediation (the "UNCITRAL Model Law on Mediation") should be considered (such as the signing of the settlement agreement by the parties, and providing evidence that the settlement agreement resulted from mediation).

41. Furthermore, parties should not commence nor continue any other international investment dispute resolution proceeding relating to all or parts of the dispute subject to mediation, to the extent the dispute had been resolved.

M. Fostering the use of mediation

42. Sections B to L explain how mediation can be used to resolve international investment disputes. States wishing to facilitate the use of mediation as a means to resolve investment disputes may consider removing impediments to its use, so that investors and States alike can effectively participate in mediation. These include providing an enabling domestic and international legal framework as well as, to the extent possible, building the capacity of those expected to participate in mediation (see para. 47 below). States may also consider mediation as a component of dispute prevention and mitigation framework.

43. *Domestic legal framework.* A legal basis in domestic law referring to the State's approval of mediation as a tool to settle disputes, including international investment disputes, would signal the possibility to use mediation to investors. Such a legal basis may also create an enabling environment for States and State entities to participate in mediation and address possible concerns of Government officials, for example, those arising from the fear of personal liability or of being accused of corruption. Such a legislation may also clarify lines of authority, representation of the State in formal or informal dispute resolution processes, and other matters.

44. When providing a domestic legal framework for enabling mediation, States may wish to consider the adoption of the UNCITRAL Model Law on Mediation, which provides for uniform rules in respect of the mediation process and aims at encouraging the use of mediation and ensuring greater predictability and certainty in its use.[17]

International legal framework

45. *Singapore Convention.* As noted (see para. 40 above), the need to enforce a settlement agreement may not arise often as parties are expected to abide by the terms therein. However, the availability of an enforcement mechanism is an element to be taken into account when choosing the most suitable dispute resolution mechanism. A State adopting the UNCITRAL Model Law on Mediation would recognize the binding and enforceable nature of a settlement agreement (see art. 15) and would ensure that the agreement is enforced by its courts (see art. 18). When it comes to cross-border enforcement of settlement agreements, the Singapore Convention is one tool for parties to enforce settlement agreements in the courts of a State party to the

---

[17] States that have enacted legislation based on the UNCITRAL Model Law on Mediation are listed at https://uncitral.un.org/en/texts/arbitration/modellaw/commercial_conciliation/status.

Convention.[18] The parties should take note of any declaration made by States parties in accordance with article 8, paragraph 1(a) of the Singapore Convention, stating that the State shall not apply the Singapore Convention to settlement agreements to which it is a party.[19]

46. *Mediation clauses in investment treaties and investment contracts.* States might include provisions in their investment treaties[20] or investment contracts to make mediation available. This may be prior to, during or after an adversarial proceeding (including in an enforcement proceeding), in other words, at any time during the life cycle of an investment. Provisions that highlight the availability of mediation would encourage parties to consider engaging in mediation. States might alternatively consider mandating the commencement of mediation to promote early constructive dialogue and to require that mediation be conducted for a certain period of time or until a certain stage.

47. *Awareness-raising and training.* Raising awareness about mediation as a tool to resolve international investment disputes and its potential benefits can further foster the use of mediation. In this regard, training and capacity-building of Government officials, as well as mediators, and other relevant target groups could be offered on a regular basis.

[18] The list of States parties to the Singapore Convention is available at https://treaties.un.org/Pages/ViewDetails.aspx?src=TREATY&mtdsg_no=XXII-4&chapter=22&clang=_en.

[19] The list of States parties to the Singapore Convention that made such declarations is available at https://treaties.un.org/Pages/ViewDetails.aspx?src=TREATY&mtdsg_no=XXII-4&chapter=22&clang=_en.

[20] See the UNCITRAL Model Provisions on Mediation for International Investment Disputes.

Annex III

UNCITRAL Code of Conduct for Arbitrators in International Investment Dispute Resolution

Article 1
Definitions

For the purposes of the Code:

(a) "International investment dispute (IID)" means a dispute between an investor and a State or a regional economic integration organization or any constituent subdivision of a State or agency of a State or a regional economic integration organization submitted for resolution pursuant to an instrument of consent;

(b) "Instrument of consent" means:

(i) A treaty providing for the protection of investments or investors;

(ii) Legislation governing foreign investments; or

(iii) An investment contract between a foreign investor and a State or a regional economic integration organization or any constituent subdivision of a State or agency of a State or a regional economic integration organization,

upon which the consent to arbitrate is based;

(c) "Arbitrator" means a person who is a member of an arbitral tribunal or an International Centre for Settlement of Investment Disputes (ICSID) ad hoc Committee, who is appointed to resolve an IID;

(d) "Candidate" means a person who has been contacted regarding a potential appointment as an Arbitrator, but who has not yet been appointed;

(e) "Ex parte communication" means any communication concerning the IID by a Candidate or an Arbitrator with a disputing party, its legal representative, affiliate, subsidiary or other related person, without the presence or knowledge of the other disputing party or its legal representative;

(f) "Applicable rules" means the applicable arbitration rules and any law applicable to the IID proceeding; and

(g) "Assistant" means a person who is working under the direction and control of an Arbitrator to assist with case-specific tasks.

Article 2
Application of the Code

1. The Code applies to an Arbitrator in, or a Candidate for, an IID proceeding, or a former Arbitrator. The Code may be applied in any other dispute resolution proceeding by agreement of the disputing parties.

2. If the instrument of consent contains provisions on the conduct of an Arbitrator, a Candidate or a former Arbitrator, the Code shall complement such provisions. In the event of any incompatibility between the Code and such provisions, the latter shall prevail to the extent of the incompatibility.

Article 3
Independence and impartiality

1. An Arbitrator shall be independent and impartial.

2. Paragraph 1 includes the obligation not to:

(a) Be influenced by loyalty to any disputing party or any other person or entity;

(b) Take instruction from any organization, government or individual regarding any matter addressed in the IID proceeding;

(c) Be influenced by any past, present or prospective financial, business, professional or personal relationship;

(d) Use his or her position to advance any financial or personal interest he or she has in any disputing party or in the outcome of the IID proceeding;

(e) Assume any function or accept any benefit that would interfere with the performance of his or her duties; or

(f) Take any action that creates the appearance of a lack of independence or impartiality.

Article 4
Limit on multiple roles

1. Unless the disputing parties agree otherwise, an Arbitrator shall not act concurrently as a legal representative or an expert witness in any other proceeding involving:

(a) The same measure(s);

(b) The same or related party (parties); or

(c) The same provision(s) of the same instrument of consent.

2. For a period of three years, a former Arbitrator shall not act as a legal representative or an expert witness in any other IID or related proceeding involving the same measure(s) unless the disputing parties agree otherwise.

3. For a period of three years, a former Arbitrator shall not act as a legal representative or an expert witness in any other IID or related proceeding involving the same or related party (parties) unless the disputing parties agree otherwise.

4. For a period of one year, a former Arbitrator shall not act as a legal representative or an expert witness in any other IID or related proceeding involving the same provision(s) of the same instrument of consent unless the disputing parties agree otherwise.

Article 5
Duty of diligence

An Arbitrator shall:

(a) Perform his or her duties diligently;

(b) Devote sufficient time to the IID proceeding; and

(c) Render all decisions in a timely manner.

Article 6
Integrity and competence

An Arbitrator shall:

(a) Conduct the IID proceeding competently and in accordance with high standards of integrity, fairness and civility;

(b) Possess the necessary competence and skills and make all reasonable efforts to maintain and enhance the knowledge, skills and qualities necessary to perform his or her duties; and

(c) Not delegate his or her decision-making function.

Article 7
Ex parte communication

1. Unless permitted by the instrument of consent, the applicable rules, agreement of the disputing parties or paragraph 2, ex parte communication is prohibited.

2. Ex parte communication is permitted when a Candidate engages in a communication with a disputing party that has contacted him or her regarding a potential appointment as a party-appointed Arbitrator for the purpose of determining the Candidate's expertise, experience, competence, skills, availability and the existence of any potential conflict of interest.

3. When permitted under this article, ex parte communication shall not, in any case, address any procedural or substantive issues relating to the IID proceeding or those that a Candidate or an Arbitrator can reasonably anticipate would arise in the IID proceeding.

Article 8
Confidentiality

1. Unless permitted by the instrument of consent, the applicable rules or agreement of the disputing parties, a Candidate, an Arbitrator or a former Arbitrator shall not:

(a) Disclose or use any information concerning, or acquired in connection with, the IID proceeding; or

(b) Disclose any draft decision in the IID proceeding.

2. An Arbitrator or a former Arbitrator shall not disclose the contents of the deliberations in the IID proceeding.

3. An Arbitrator or a former Arbitrator may comment on a decision rendered in the IID proceeding only if it was made publicly available in accordance with the instrument of consent or the applicable rules.

4. Notwithstanding paragraph 3, an Arbitrator or a former Arbitrator shall not comment on a decision while the IID proceeding is pending or the decision is subject to a post-award remedy or review.

5. The obligations in this article shall not apply to the extent that a Candidate, an Arbitrator or a former Arbitrator is legally compelled to disclose the information in a court or other competent body or needs to disclose such information to protect or pursue his or her legal rights or in relation to legal proceedings before a court or other competent body.

Article 9
Fees and expenses

1. Fees and expenses of an Arbitrator shall be reasonable and in accordance with the instrument of consent or the applicable rules.

2. Any discussion concerning fees and expenses shall be concluded with the disputing parties as soon as possible.

3. Any proposal concerning fees and expenses shall be communicated to the disputing parties through the institution administering the proceeding. If there is no administering institution, such proposal shall be communicated to the disputing parties by the sole or presiding Arbitrator.

4. An Arbitrator shall keep an accurate record of his or her time and expenses attributable to the IID proceeding and shall make such records available when requesting the disbursement of funds or upon the request of a disputing party.

Article 10
Assistant

1 Prior to engaging an Assistant, an Arbitrator shall agree with the disputing parties on the role, scope of duties and fees and expenses of his or her Assistant.

2. An Arbitrator shall make all reasonable efforts to ensure that his or her Assistant is aware of and acts in accordance with the Code, including by requiring the Assistant to sign a declaration to that effect, and shall remove an Assistant who does not act in accordance with the Code.

3. An Arbitrator shall ensure that the Assistant keeps an accurate record of his or her time and expenses attributable to the IID proceeding.

Article 11
Disclosure obligations

1 A Candidate and an Arbitrator shall disclose any circumstances likely to give rise to justifiable doubts as to his or her independence or impartiality.

2. Regardless of whether required under paragraph 1, the following information shall be disclosed:

(a) Any financial, business, professional or close personal relationship in the past five years with:

(i) Any disputing party;

(ii) The legal representative of a disputing party in the IID proceeding;

(iii) Other Arbitrators and expert witnesses in the IID proceeding; and

(iv) Any person or entity identified by a disputing party as being related or as having a direct or indirect interest in the outcome of the IID proceeding, including a third-party funder;

(b) Any financial or personal interest in:

(i) The outcome of the IID proceeding;

(ii) Any other proceeding involving the same measure(s); and

(iii) Any other proceeding involving a disputing party or a person or entity identified by a disputing party as being related;

(c) All IID and related proceedings in which the Candidate or the Arbitrator is currently or has been involved in the past five years as an Arbitrator, a legal representative or an expert witness;

(d) Any appointment as an Arbitrator, a legal representative or an expert witness by a disputing party or its legal representative in an IID or any other proceeding in the past five years; and

(e) Any prospective concurrent appointment as a legal representative or an expert witness in any other IID or related proceeding.

3. An Arbitrator shall have a continuing duty to make further disclosures based on new or newly discovered circumstances and information as soon as he or she becomes aware of such circumstances and information.

4. For the purposes of paragraphs 1 to 3, a Candidate and an Arbitrator shall make all reasonable efforts to become aware of such circumstances and information.

5. A Candidate and an Arbitrator shall err in favour of disclosure if he or she has any doubt as to whether a disclosure shall be made.

6. If a Candidate or an Arbitrator is bound by confidentiality obligations and cannot disclose all of the required circumstances or information in this article, he or she shall make the disclosure to the extent possible. If a Candidate or an Arbitrator is unable to disclose circumstances that are likely to give rise to justifiable doubts as to his or her independence or impartiality, he or she shall not accept the appointment or shall resign or recuse himself or herself from the IID proceeding.

7. A Candidate and an Arbitrator shall make the disclosure prior to or upon appointment to the disputing parties, other Arbitrators in the IID proceeding, any administering institution and any other persons prescribed by the instrument of consent or the applicable rules.

8. The fact of non-disclosure does not in itself necessarily establish a lack of independence or impartiality.

Article 12
Compliance with the Code

1. An Arbitrator, a former Arbitrator and a Candidate shall comply with the Code.

2. A Candidate shall not accept an appointment and an Arbitrator shall resign or recuse himself or herself from the IID proceeding if he or she is not able to comply with the Code.

3. Any challenge or disqualification of an Arbitrator or any other sanction or remedy is governed by the instrument of consent or the applicable rules.

Annex 1 (Candidates/Arbitrators)

Declaration, disclosure and background information

1. I have read and understood the attached UNCITRAL Code of Conduct for Arbitrators in International Investment Dispute Resolution (the "Code of Conduct") and I undertake to comply with it.

2. To the best of my knowledge, there is no reason why I should not serve as an Arbitrator in this proceeding. I am impartial and independent and have no impediment arising from the Code of Conduct.

3. I attach my current curriculum vitae to this declaration.

4. In accordance with article 11 of the Code of Conduct, I wish to make the following disclosure and provide the following information:

[*Insert relevant information*]

5. I confirm that as of the date of this declaration, I have no further circumstance or information to disclose. I shall make further disclosures based on new or newly discovered circumstances and information as soon as I become aware of such circumstances and information.

Annex 2 (Assistants)

Declaration

1. I have read and understood the attached UNCITRAL Code of Conduct for Arbitrators in International Investment Dispute Resolution (the "Code of Conduct") and I undertake to act in accordance with it.

2. I confirm that at the date of this declaration, I am not aware of any circumstance that would preclude me from acting in accordance with the Code of Conduct.

Annex IV

UNCITRAL Code of Conduct for Judges in International Investment Dispute Resolution

Article 1
Definitions

For the purposes of the Code:

(a) "Judge" means a person who is a member of a standing mechanism;

(b) "Candidate" means a person who is under consideration for appointment as a Judge, but who has not yet been confirmed in such role; and

(c) "Ex parte communication" means any communication concerning a proceeding before a standing mechanism by a Judge with a disputing party, its legal representative, affiliate, subsidiary or other related person, without the presence or knowledge of the other disputing party or its legal representative.

Article 2
Application of the Code

The Code applies to a Judge, a Candidate or a former Judge in accordance with the rules of the standing mechanism.

Article 3
Independence and impartiality

1. A Judge shall be independent and impartial.

2. Paragraph 1 includes the obligation not to:

(a) Be influenced by loyalty to any disputing party or any other person or entity;

(b) Take instruction from any organization, government or individual regarding any matter addressed in a proceeding before the standing mechanism;

(c) Be influenced by any past, present or prospective financial, business, professional or personal relationship;

(d) Use his or her position to advance any financial or personal interest he or she has in any disputing party, or in the outcome of a proceeding, before the standing mechanism;

(e) Assume any function or accept any benefit that would interfere with the performance of his or her duties; or

(f) Take any action that creates the appearance of a lack of independence or impartiality.

Article 4
Limit on multiple roles

1. A Judge shall not exercise any political or administrative function. He or she shall not engage in any other occupation of a professional nature which is incompatible with his or her obligation of independence and impartiality or with the demands of the terms of office. In particular, a Judge shall not act as a legal representative or an expert witness in any other proceeding.

2. A Judge shall declare any other function or occupation in accordance with the rules of the standing mechanism. Any question regarding paragraph 1 shall be settled by the standing mechanism.

3. A former Judge shall not become involved in any manner in any proceeding before the standing mechanism, which was pending during his or her term of office.

4. A former Judge shall not act as a legal representative or an expert witness in any proceeding before the standing mechanism for a period of three years following the end of his or her term of office.

Article 5
Duty of diligence

A Judge shall perform the duties of his or her office diligently in accordance with the terms of office.

Article 6
Integrity and competence

A Judge shall:

(a) Conduct proceedings competently and in accordance with high standards of integrity, fairness and civility;

(b) Possess the necessary competence and skills and make all reasonable efforts to maintain and enhance the knowledge, skills and qualities necessary to perform his or her duties; and

(c) Not delegate his or her decision-making function.

Article 7
Ex parte communication

Unless permitted by the rules of the standing mechanism, ex parte communication is prohibited.

Article 8
Confidentiality

1. Unless permitted by the rules of the standing mechanism, a Judge or a former Judge shall not:

(a) Disclose or use any information concerning, or acquired in connection with, a proceeding before the standing mechanism;

(b) Disclose any draft decision in a proceeding before the standing mechanism; or

(c) Disclose the contents of the deliberations in a proceeding before the standing mechanism.

2. Unless permitted by the rules of the standing mechanism, a Judge shall not comment on a decision rendered in a proceeding before the standing mechanism, and a former Judge shall not comment on a decision rendered in a proceeding before the standing mechanism for a period of three years following the end of his or her term of office.

3. The obligations in this article shall not apply to the extent that a Judge or a former Judge is legally compelled to disclose the information in a court or other competent body or needs to disclose such information to protect or pursue his or her legal rights or in relation to legal proceedings before a court or other competent body.

Article 9
Disclosure obligations

1. A Candidate and a Judge shall disclose any circumstances likely to give rise to justifiable doubts as to his or her independence or impartiality.

2. Regardless of whether required under paragraph 1, a Candidate shall disclose all proceedings in which the Candidate is currently or has been involved in the past five years, including as an arbitrator, a legal representative or an expert witness.

3. Regardless of whether required under paragraph 1, the following information shall be disclosed by a Judge with regard to a proceeding which he or she is expected to adjudicate or is adjudicating:

(a) Any financial, business, professional or close personal relationship in the past five years with:

(i) Any disputing party in the proceeding;

(ii) The legal representative of a disputing party in the proceeding;

(iii) Expert witnesses in the proceeding; and

(iv) Any person or entity identified by a disputing party as being related or as having a direct or indirect interest in the outcome of the proceeding, including a third-party funder; and

(b) Any financial or personal interest in:

(i) The outcome of the proceeding;

(ii) Any other proceeding involving the same measure or measures; and

(iii) Any other proceeding involving a disputing party or a person or entity identified by a disputing party as being related.

4. For the purposes of paragraphs 1 to 3, a Candidate and a Judge shall make all reasonable efforts to become aware of such circumstances and information.

5. A Candidate shall make the disclosure to the standing mechanism in accordance with the rules of the standing mechanism.

6. A Judge shall make the disclosure in accordance with the rules of the standing mechanism as soon as he or she becomes aware of the circumstances and information mentioned in paragraphs 1 and 3. A Judge shall have a continuing duty to make further disclosures based on new or newly discovered circumstances and information.

7. A Candidate and a Judge shall err in favour of disclosure if he or she has any doubt as to whether a disclosure shall be made.

8. The fact of non-disclosure does not in itself necessarily establish a lack of independence or impartiality.

Article 10
Compliance with the Code

Compliance with the Code shall be governed by the rules of the standing mechanism.

Annex 1 (Candidates)

Declaration, disclosure and background information

1. I have read and understood the attached UNCITRAL Code of Conduct for Judges in International Investment Dispute Resolution (the "Code of Conduct") and I undertake to comply with it.

2. To the best of my knowledge, there is no reason why I should not serve as a Judge and I have no impediment arising from the Code of Conduct.

3. In accordance with article 9 of the Code of Conduct, I wish to make the following disclosure and provide the following information:

[*Insert relevant information*]

4. I confirm that as of the date of this declaration, I have no further circumstance or information to disclose. I understand that I shall make further disclosures based on new or newly discovered circumstances and information as soon as I become aware of such circumstances and information.

Annex 2 (Judges)

Declaration and disclosure

1. I have read and understood the attached UNCITRAL Code of Conduct for Judges in International Investment Dispute Resolution (the "Code of Conduct") and I undertake to comply with it.

2. To the best of my knowledge, there is no reason why I should not serve as a Judge. I am impartial and independent and have no impediment arising from the Code of Conduct.

3. In accordance with article 9 of the Code of Conduct, I wish to make the following disclosure and provide the following information:

[*Insert relevant information*]

4. I confirm that as of the date of this declaration, I have no further circumstance or information to disclose. I understand that I shall make further disclosures based on new or newly discovered circumstances and information as soon as I become aware of such circumstances and information.

Annex V

Recommendations on Access to Credit for Micro-, Small and Medium-sized Enterprises

Recommendation 1

The law should ensure that micro-, small and medium-sized enterprises (MSMEs) have access to credit without discrimination based on any ground such as race, colour, gender, marital status, language, religion, political or other opinion, national or social origin, property, birth, disability or other status.

Recommendation 2

The law should ensure that:

(a) Women have equal and enforceable rights of access to credit in order to start and operate a business; and

(b) The requirements for access to credit do not discriminate against potential borrowers based on their gender.

Recommendation 3

To facilitate access to credit, the law should promote the formation of businesses, including MSMEs, in the formal economy by providing for an efficient and simplified system of business registration such as that described in the *UNCITRAL Legislative Guide on Key Principles of a Business Registry*.

Recommendation 4

To facilitate access to credit by enabling the participation of MSMEs in the formal economy, the law should provide for simplified organizational forms for MSMEs, such as the form recommended in the *UNCITRAL Legislative Guide on Limited Liability Enterprises*.

Recommendation 5

To enable MSMEs to utilize movable assets as collateral:

(a) The law should provide for a modern and comprehensive secured transactions regime in accordance with the *UNCITRAL Model Law on Secured Transactions*;

(b) The secured transactions regime should:

(i) Facilitate the easy creation of security rights in movable assets;

(ii) Provide for the creation of security rights in future assets;

(iii) Ensure that a security right can easily be made effective against third parties by registration of a notice;

(iv) Enable creditors to determine the priority of their security rights when entering into the transaction by referring to the registry; and

(v) Enable simple and economically efficient realization on the collateral in the event of default; and

(c) The secured transactions regime should apply to all transactions in which movable assets are provided as collateral to secure payment or other performance of an obligation, including those in which the creditor retains title to an asset or title to an asset is transferred to the creditor in order to secure an obligation, and regardless of whether the parties have denominated the creditor's right as a security right.

Recommendation 6

The law should provide for a secured transactions regime with respect to immovable assets which allows:

(a) The creation of security rights over all types of immovable assets by all types of persons to secure all types of obligations;

(b) The determination of the priority of the secured creditor's rights when entering into the transaction; and

(c) The realization of security rights over immovable assets.

Recommendation 7

To help ensure that guarantors and financers of MSMEs are aware of their rights and obligations, the law should:

(a) Require the terms and conditions of the guarantee to be clear, understandable and legible; and

(b) Identify both the formalities and content requirements necessary to make a guarantee effective.

Recommendation 8

To enable financers to more accurately assess the creditworthiness of MSMEs that are potential borrowers, the law should:

(a) Establish a legal and regulatory framework for the creation and operation of public or private commercial credit reporting systems; and

(b) Specify the nature and scope of reporting obligations with respect to such systems.

Recommendation 9

In order to address the financial needs of MSMEs in the context of insolvency, the law should reflect international standards such as those found in the *UNCITRAL Legislative Guide on Insolvency Law* and the *UNCITRAL Legislative Guide on Insolvency Law for Micro- and Small Enterprises*.

Recommendation 10

To help ensure that MSMEs are aware of their rights and obligations, the law should require the terms and conditions of the credit agreement to be presented by financers to MSMEs in a clear, understandable and legible way.

Recommendation 11

The law should identify both the formalities and content requirements necessary to make a credit agreement effective, taking into account the interest of the MSME in understanding the obligation it is incurring and in the avoidance of unfair terms or practices.

Recommendation 12

States should further enhance the legal and policy measures supporting access to credit for MSMEs with relevant programmes and policies for improving the legal and financial literacy of MSMEs and the capacity of financers and regulators.

Annex VI

Programme of the Colloquium on Climate Change and International Trade Law

Time	*Activity*
Wednesday, 12 July 2023	
9 a.m.	Registration of participants
9.30 a.m.	**Opening of the Colloquium** by the Chair of UNCITRAL at its fifty-sixth session **Welcome address and introduction** by Nicola Murray, Deputy Permanent Representative of the Mission of the United Kingdom of Great Britain and Northern Ireland to the United Nations and other International Organisations in Vienna and the Secretary of UNCITRAL
9.40 a.m.	**1. The role of market mechanisms under the international framework on climate change** This session will provide a general overview of the international framework for climate action under the Kyoto Protocol and the Paris Agreement, with a focus on the role envisaged for the private sector, in particular through market mechanisms for emission reduction and the promotion of clean investment. Moderator: Holger Federico Martinsen, Ambassador Extraordinary and Plenipotentiary, Permanent Mission of Argentina to the United Nations (Vienna) Keynote speech: Annette L. Nazareth, Chair, Integrity Council for the Voluntary Carbon Market (ICVCM) Speakers: • Phillip Eyre, Team Lead of the Markets and Non-markets Support Unit, Mitigation Division, United Nations Framework Convention on Climate Change (UNFCCC) • Søren Lütken, Senior Economist, Copenhagen Climate Centre, United Nations Environment Programme (UNEP) • Thomas Clark, General Counsel, Asian Development Bank (ADB)
10.45 a.m.	Coffee break
11 a.m.	**2. Financial instruments to support emission reduction and carbon trading: regulatory aspects and legal underpinnings** This session will discuss financial instruments for green investment, focusing on business models for issuance, intermediation and custodianship, as well as regulatory and legal aspects, to ensure interoperability, promote integrity and enhance legal certainty for emission trading system schemes. Moderator: Ignacio Tirado, Secretary-General, UNIDROIT Speakers: • Dirk Forrister, CEO, International Emissions Trading Association • Flavia Rosembuj, Programme Manager for the Partnership for Market Implementation, Climate Change Group, World Bank • Bénédicte Nolens, Head of the Hong Kong Innovation Hub, Bank for International Settlements (Hong Kong, China) • Peter Werner, Senior Counsel, International Swaps and Derivatives Association

Time	*Activity*
12.15 p.m.	Open discussion
12.30 p.m.	Lunch
2 p.m.	**3. Green investment certification and compliance** This session will discuss certification and compliance methods for promoting confidence in green investment and preventing "greenwashing". Moderator: Wendy Miles KC, Barrister, Twenty Essex (London) and Representative, Net Zero Lawyers Alliance Speakers: • Gabriela Rodríguez Martínez, Senior Adviser for Sustainable Policies and Finance, International Affairs Unit, Ministry of Finance and Public Credit of Mexico • Kris Nathanail, Senior Policy Advisor for Special Projects, International Organization of Securities Commissions (IOSCO) • Mauricio Moura Costa, Co-Founder and CEO, BVRio (Rio de Janeiro, Brazil) • Tatiana C. Alves, Sector Lead Specialist, Green Finance, Connectivity, Markets and Finance Division, Inter-American Development Bank
3.15 p.m.	**Open discussion**
3.30 p.m.	**Coffee break**
3.45 p.m.	**4. Green bonds and carbon credits as financial instruments: legal nature, trading and holding patterns** The session will discuss the legal nature of voluntary carbon credits and other green investment instruments, their use as collateral and the rights of holders. Moderator: José Angelo Estrella-Faria, Principal Legal Officer, UNCITRAL Speakers: • Géraud de Lassus St-Geniès, Professor of Law, Laval University (Quebec, Canada) • Xiaoping Zhang, Associate Professor of Law, Central University of Finance and Economics (Beijing) • Tatiana C. Alves, Sector Lead Specialist, Green Finance Connectivity, Markets and Finance Division, Inter-American Development Bank • Lisa DeMarco, Chair of the Board, International Emission Trading Association
4.45 p.m.	**Open discussion**
5 p.m.	**Closing of Day 1**
Thursday, 13 July 2023	
9 a.m.	**Registration of participants and opening of the second day**
9.30 a.m.	**5. Corporate social responsibility, due diligence and disclosure of climate impact** This session will focus on the international, regional and States' efforts to call upon private sector support towards achieving climate goals by advocating and advancing climate-responsible corporate conduct. The discussion will touch upon, among others, existing international instruments and regional and domestic legislations aimed at increasing transparency and accountability for climate impact of business models and investment strategies through due diligence and information disclosure.

Time	*Activity*
	Moderator: José Angelo Estrella Faria, Principal Legal Officer, UNCITRAL Speakers: • Tihana Bule, Head of Governance and Multilateral Relations, Centre for Responsible Business Conduct, Organisation for Economic Co-operation and Development • Meng Su, Partner, King and Wood Mallesons (Shanghai, China) • Vesselina Haralampieva, Senior Counsel, European Bank for Reconstruction and Development • Katharina Bryan, Head of Sustainability Reporting Policy, European Union and International, Amazon (Luxembourg)
11 a.m.	**Open discussion**
11.15 a.m.	**6. Greening the supply chain: contractual and liability enforcement mechanisms** This session will discuss the various adaptation strategies and approaches available to private sector operators to promote sustainability in their supply chains, especially through incorporating corresponding contractual and liability enforcement mechanisms into existing commercial practices. Moderator: Stéphane Wohlfahrt, Senior Legal Officer, UNCITRAL Speakers: • Yeşim M. Atamer, Professor of Law, University of Zurich (Zurich, Switzerland) • Christian Richter-Schöller, Co-head of Sustainability Group, DORDA (Vienna, Austria) • Ipshita Chaturvedi, Partner, Dentons Rodyk (Singapore)
12.15 p.m.	**Open discussion**
12.30 p.m.	**Lunch**
2 p.m.	**7. Climate change dispute resolution** The aim of the session is to explore and evaluate the current trends in climate change disputes and their legal implication for corporates to fulfil the duty of care and foster the incorporation of climate considerations into business and investment decision. Moderator: Jae-Sung Lee, Senior Legal Officer, UNCITRAL Speakers: • Wendy Miles KC, Barrister, Twenty Essex (London) and Representative, Net Zero Lawyers Alliance • Annette Magnusson, Co-Founder, Climate Change Counsel (Stockholm, Sweden) • Aisha Abdallah, Partner, Head of Litigation and Disputes, Anjarwalla and Khanna (Nairobi, Kenya) • Tomoko Ishikawa, Vice Dean, Graduate School of International Development Nagoya University (Nagoya, Japan)
3.15 p.m.	**Open discussion**
3.30 p.m.	**Coffee break**

Time	Activity
3.45 p.m.	**8. High-level member States round table: Possible work by UNCITRAL on climate change and private law** The aim of the session is to assess, on the basis of the preceding sessions, the feasibility and desirability of work by UNCITRAL on climate change and private law and, if work were to be undertaken, its possible form and scope. Moderator: Chair, fifty-sixth session of UNCITRAL Participants: Permanent representatives to Vienna-based organizations Armenia Armen Papikyan Ambassador Extraordinary and Plenipotentiary Morocco Azzeddine Farhane Ambassador Extraordinary and Plenipotentiary Paraguay Juan Francisco Facetti Fernandez Ambassador Extraordinary and Plenipotentiary Thailand Vilawan Mangklatanakul Ambassador Extraordinary and Plenipotentiary
4.45 p.m.	**Open discussion**
5 p.m.	**Closing of the Colloquium**

Annex VII

UNCITRAL Notes on Organizing Arbitral Proceedings – Note 21. Early dismissal and preliminary determination

21. Early dismissal and preliminary determination

147. Many arbitration rules provide discretion to the arbitral tribunal to conduct the arbitration in a manner it considers appropriate provided that the parties are treated with equality and that each party is given a reasonable opportunity to present its case. In exercising the discretion, the arbitral tribunal should conduct the proceedings in a manner that avoids unnecessary delay and expense and provide a fair and efficient process for resolving the parties' dispute. One such discretionary power is the ability of the arbitral tribunal to dismiss a claim or defence on the ground that it is manifestly without merit or that the arbitral tribunal manifestly lacks jurisdiction, or to make a preliminary determination to that effect (referred to below as "early dismissal"). This includes the early dismissal of a counterclaim and a claim for the purposes of set-off.

148. The exercise of such discretionary power for early dismissal depends on the circumstances and the applicable arbitration rules. One possible approach is to implement an early dismissal process. Under an early dismissal process, if a request for early dismissal of any claim or defence is made by a party, it should be raised as promptly as possible. In considering such a request or in initiating the process on its own initiative, the arbitral tribunal shall invite the parties to express their views.

149. When determining whether to proceed with the early dismissal process, the arbitral tribunal should take into account a number of factors including the stage of the proceedings. For example, if the arbitral tribunal considers that the early dismissal process may lead to unnecessary delay and expense, or may undermine a fair and efficient process, it may decide not to proceed. The arbitral tribunal would usually require the party making the request to provide justifying grounds and may require that party to demonstrate that the early dismissal process will expedite the overall proceeding. This could prevent a request for early dismissal from being misused by the parties to delay the proceedings.

150. Provisions of the applicable arbitration laws or arbitration rules usually recognize the arbitral tribunal's authority to rule on its own jurisdiction and allow parties to raise any objection on jurisdiction. The standard and timing for considering the objection under those provisions are not affected by the arbitral tribunal's ability to decide that it manifestly lacks jurisdiction as a matter of early dismissal.

151. Upon determining that the early dismissal process would proceed, the arbitral tribunal should invite the parties to express their views and indicate the procedure it will follow, possibly indicating a period of time within which it will make a ruling. Such a period should be reasonably short. The arbitral tribunal should ensure that parties have a reasonable opportunity to prepare and present their case.

152. The arbitral tribunal should make a ruling as soon as practicable and within the indicated period of time. Depending on the nature of the ruling and its impact on the proceeding, the arbitral tribunal may not need to continue the proceedings or examine all other issues of the case.

153. A ruling on early dismissal may take the form of an order or an award depending on the circumstances. For example, if the arbitral tribunal decides to deny the request, it may issue an order to that effect. If the arbitral tribunal decides that a claim or a defence is manifestly without merit and there are other claims or defences remaining, the arbitral tribunal may issue a partial award. The arbitral tribunal would then continue with the proceedings to consider the remaining claims. If the arbitral tribunal decides that all the claims are manifestly without merit, the arbitral tribunal may issue a final award to that effect or may order the termination of the proceeding.

154. The arbitral tribunal should provide reasons when making a ruling. If such reasoning is not required under the applicable arbitration law, parties may agree that no reasons are to be given.

Annex VIII

List of documents before the Commission at its fifty-sixth session

Symbol	*Title or description*
A/CN.9/1121	Provisional agenda, annotations thereto and scheduling of meetings of the fifty-sixth session
A/CN.9/1122	Report of Working Group I (MSMEs) on the work of its thirty-eighth session
A/CN.9/1123	Report of Working Group II (Dispute Settlement) on the work of its seventy-sixth session
A/CN.9/1124	Report of Working Group III (Investor-State Dispute Settlement Reform) on the work of its forty-third session
A/CN.9/1125	Report of Working Group IV (Electronic Commerce) on the work of its sixty-fourth session
A/CN.9/1126	Report of Working Group V (Insolvency Law) on the work of its sixty-first session
A/CN.9/1127	Report of Working Group VI (Negotiable Multimodal Transport Documents) on the work of its forty-first session
A/CN.9/1128	Report of Working Group I (Micro-, Small and Medium-sized Enterprises) on the work of its thirty-ninth session
A/CN.9/1129	Report of Working Group II (Dispute Settlement) on the work of its seventy-seventh session
A/CN.9/1130	Report of Working Group III (Investor-State Dispute Settlement Reform) on the work of its forty-fourth session
A/CN.9/1131	Report of Working Group III (Investor-State Dispute Settlement Reform) on the work of its forty-fifth session
A/CN.9/1132	Report of Working Group IV (Electronic Commerce) on the work of its sixty-fifth session
A/CN.9/1133	Report of Working Group V (Insolvency Law) on the work of its sixty-second session
A/CN.9/1134	Report of Working Group VI (Negotiable Multimodal Transport Documents) on the work of its forty-second session
A/CN.9/1135	Bibliography of recent writings related to the work of UNCITRAL
A/CN.9/1136	Status of conventions and model laws and the operation of the Transparency Registry
A/CN.9/1137	UNCITRAL regional presence: activities of the UNCITRAL Regional Centre for Asia and the Pacific
A/CN.9/1138	Technical cooperation and assistance
A/CN.9/1139	Dissemination of information and related activities to support the UNCITRAL's work and the use of its texts, including report on CLOUT and Digests
A/CN.9/1140	Work programme of the Commission
A/CN.9/1141/Rev.1	Relevant General Assembly resolutions

Symbol	*Title or description*
A/CN.9/1142	Coordination and cooperation: international governmental and non-governmental organizations invited to sessions of UNCITRAL and its working groups
A/CN.9/1143	Coordination activities
A/CN.9/1144	Exploratory work on the impact of COVID-19 on international trade law
A/CN.9/1145	Early dismissal and preliminary determination
A/CN.9/1146	Legal issues relating to the use of distributed ledger technology in trade: scoping paper
A/CN.9/1147/Rev.1	Role of UNCITRAL in promoting the rule of law at the national and international levels
A/CN.9/1148	Draft code of conduct for arbitrators in international investment dispute resolution and commentary
A/CN.9/1149	Draft code of conduct for judges in international investment dispute resolution and commentary
A/CN.9/1150	Draft provisions on mediation
A/CN.9/1151	Draft UNCITRAL guidelines on investment mediation
A/CN.9/1152	Work programme: warehouse receipts
A/CN.9/1153	Work programme: possible future work on climate change mitigation, adaptation and resilience
A/CN.9/1153/Add.1	Work programme: possible future work on climate change mitigation, adaptation and resilience
A/CN.9/1154	Stocktaking of developments in dispute resolution in the digital economy
A/CN.9/1155	Stocktaking of developments in dispute resolution in the digital economy
A/CN.9/1156	Draft guide on access to credit for micro-, small and medium-sized enterprises (MSMEs)